About the Author

For twelve years, Bronwen Kalea lived off the grid on a mountain farm in the beautiful hinterland of the Mid North Coast, Australia. She shared her rustic lifestyle with a cat, dogs, goats, geese, chooks and her beloved horses. She is mother to a university striving daughter and a secondary school English teacher who loves the magic of storytelling, especially when it centres around human development, the mysterious and Mother Nature.

Elijah Blue Jeans

Bronwen Kalea

Elijah Blue Jeans

Vanguard Press

VANGUARD PAPERBACK

© Copyright 2024
Bronwen Kalea

The right of Bronwen Kalea to be identified as author of this work has been asserted by her in accordance with the Copyright, Designs and Patents Act 1988.

All Rights Reserved

No reproduction, copy or transmission of this publication may be made without written permission.
No paragraph of this publication may be reproduced, copied or transmitted save with the written permission of the publisher, or in accordance with the provisions of the Copyright Act 1956 (as amended).

Any person who commits any unauthorised act in relation to this publication may be liable to criminal prosecution and civil claims for damages.

A CIP catalogue record for this title is available from the British Library.

ISBN 978 1 80016 842 8

Vanguard Press is an imprint of
Pegasus Elliot Mackenzie Publishers Ltd.
www.pegasuspublishers.com

First Published in 2024

Vanguard Press
Sheraton House Castle Park
Cambridge England

Printed & Bound in Great Britain

For Elijah

Acknowledgements

Thank you to my family and friends for always being there for me—in life and in the essence of this story. Thank you to beautiful Blue Jeans for making your way to me and blessing my soul forever.

Prologue

They thundered across seasoned grounds of triumph
With hooves that split the earth to shards of Light
A vibrant mix of color, breed and passion

The ancient spur of hope known deep within them
Now speed and strength must come together

For these were the ones that were healed
And people who had passed, gathered to watch them
I was watching them

Their power and their ethereal beauty
Their manes that brushed the memory of a star
While hearts fall heavy on the understanding
That it begins
That it ends

PART 1

Chapter 1
A Country Girl

The last seven years of my life sound, feel and break down into acronym compartments like the word tumultuous. Too many utterly tough and unexpected things. Ous! If someone had shown me a map, a flow chart, or even a glimpse of what was to come my way, I may have asked for a prolonged tea break in some swish establishment on the other side of the universe. In fact, I know I would have. Truly. Like many I guess, I have recently lived some very hard times. My name is Bronwen, I am a country girl and to top it all off, I am now rather unenthusiastically approaching sixty. Yep, I am getting on.

I live off the grid on a mountain farm in Pappinbarra, New South Wales, Australia. This little rural paradise, wedged deeply into the hinterland of the Mid North Coast, is home to both hippies and farming community. I would be a decent mix of the two. I love to work and dream and dance on the glorious land. If nature had a special secret, it would be my backyard. Fifty acres of pure utopia, give or take a lantana bush or two.

I live amongst some of the best human beings on Earth. I say this because it has been proven to me over and over again. If the fence breaks, someone down the road lends a hand to fix it; if I run out of food, my best friend two mountains over somehow senses this and turns up with her latest harvest; if a fire rages unexpectedly, then the next day, so too do chainsaws, shovels, wheelbarrows and warm hugs—mates that know without a second thought, you must look after your friends when the shit really hits the fan. Bush dances, trivia nights, communal markets and fresh scones and tea from the back of a ute after church, are as dear to my log of memories as each moment in pristine wilderness.

We may live in tranquil beauty but then be shaken by life in such merciless haste. This is how it was, when *change* exceeded itself and the thump of my pounded soul, consistently broke the stillness of night.

My twenty-year marriage ended when I was just a spring chicken at fifty-one. I did not see it coming, did not handle it very well, cried a lot. During shock, grief, anger, hurt and major identity crisis, two fires hit our country paddocks. One almost took my home, my animals and managed to destroy all the essential structure I had meticulously put together over the years— which then required many more years of back-breaking labour to reinstate. There was a very long period of drought before all this occurred and I actually witnessed the lush green land beneath my bare feet turn to brown broken glass that could draw blood. Anxious, hand-picked orchard and ornamental trees that had been carefully raised up, perished. *Come up for air now, just take a moment.* There was no pause, no moment, no breather before the most wonderful, loving father, died, slowly in a hospital bed, gasping, gargling, breaking our hearts. For months, I was numb and bereft of all senses and memories, delivering flowers by horseback to the hollow of a tree in our sacred nature place across the mountains where I live. Trying to remember him while trying not to think of him.

Floods and storms followed, and a thing called Covid-19, a worldwide pandemic, that would meet me somewhere amongst the cumulative derailment. Many of the natural challenges around this time, somehow became known and conveyed in official conversation as *unprecedented*, and the word *event* got thrown around a lot too. I always thought an *event* was a road trip to the nearest city, or a night at the theatre. Now anything tough or problematic, became talked about as a health or weather *event*, akin to the latest day out, shared by the masses and the six o'clock news.

I am a one woman show, a single mum with a single child. There is zippo luck when it comes to meeting a decent fellow. Being caught in some twisted and calculated thriller with the dating app world, I am constantly confused by what God has to offer, while I am simply searching for a face. You know, the one that makes me feel that I am home. Man, I just cannot find it.

But let's get something straight, I graduated five sloggin years of university, while I worked in different jobs to keep up with the bills and manage the demands of our property. I also got my beautiful girl through high school, with all its special occasions, academic challenges and teenage heartbreaks. My daughter and I have pioneered, endured and survived. We have shared breathtakingly beautiful sunsets alongside empty water tanks, zero power, and a genuine lack of country cheer.

There were nights when I was just too damn scared to close my eyes. Our farm is on the side of *Nowhere Ridge*, we live remotely, so yep, we got a visit from those unsavoury kind of people that you wish just never existed, let alone decided to turn up in your picture. For a period, there seemed to be a succession of different visitors to the property that really rocked our sense of trust. What can I say? We dealt with it, we overcame and we got smarter and stronger.

All that said, I am very blessed. I have my health, my beautiful girl, my horses and the best job in the world teaching Secondary School English in the best school in the world. Despite all the flaming bullshit challenges, I choose *my* life!

And then there is this extra appendage—another kind of song in my soul that simply exists. It has been with me for practically my whole life and there are no signs of departure any time soon. At the far end of my fifties, I was oblivious to the fact that I was about to be met with something so unbearable, that my own heart, would simply smash against the walls of my chest. That parts of me would shatter like fine fragments of crystal, never to be whole again.

Chapter 2
The Oldest Dream

I am a horse lover. I was born that way. There is an old home movie of me at five-years-old on the back of a Shetland pony. My father had organised this birthday party surprise for a neighbourhood of excited screaming kids. When I watch the film, I remember the day and then as the little brown pony comes to a halt after his endless charitable circles, my captivated eyes look directly into the camera and I know—I am in love for life.

From that time on I began learning all about them, going to riding schools, drawing horse pictures everywhere, even galloping into my fourth-grade classroom each morning. There was a time I remember very clearly from those early years of utter devotion. I was sitting on my favourite branch of our front yard tree with my faded Levi's on, my shaggy dog haircut, my bottle green T-shirt and *Horsey*, choker necklace. I decided that one day I would raise a foal. It would be amazing to know a horse from the very beginning and this foal and I would become best friends. He was my *dream horse* and this was my special, special dream. I locked it deep into my heart and believed that it was only a matter of time.

From the age of twelve to fifty-eight, I have loved and owned ten horses. Every single horse has taught me something. I have been dragged, kicked, bucked-off, stood on, knocked over, bitten, saved, hugged, invited into the herd and thoroughly educated by hard school equine teachers. A horse is always honest. Not necessarily easy or gentle, but they will teach you their ways and their language if you are willing to keep getting up on your two legs and *pay the heck* attention.

They tell you things you do not want to hear and things that you never imagined possible. They are sensitive creatures that require sensitivity in their direction, so that trust can be formed and a rare form of kinship.

I taught my stepchildren to ride horses when they were young and my daughter, Leilani when she was ready. I have rescued three horses and been so privileged to be part of their physical and psychological healing. Learning again, witnessing the miracle of their recovery and then the combined heartbreak and joy of re-homing them. I have buried horses, put my dearest Quarter Horse down in his suffering through his twilight years and broken two horses in, now my two beautiful mares who are with me in my current country life.

It was time to start the special story. I never forgot about it, but I was not going to rush into it. It had to be thought through. How old would I be with a foal? I worked out that if I lived to ninety, we would hopefully peak at around the same time. Would I keep them? Hell, yes! I would break them in, of course and maybe one of my grandchildren would ride them one day. What about my Jess? My big Quarter Horse mare? I sat on the crooked paddock fence and called her over. It only made sense to ask her directly,

"Do you want to have a baby, girl?" I waited. The same kind of waiting I had done when asking her, do you want me to ride you soon. Jess and Shanti had both invited me to do *first ride*. It is hard to explain how this happens with a horse, but it does.

Some people call it whispering, but it is more listening than saying anything. A horse can talk to you from the inside. A bit like telepathy, but it includes the heart of you. You hear them. You just cannot not hear them, when they want to communicate in this way. Their strong, booming voices reverberate through your chest and ears, stirring all your senses. You look around, wondering if anybody else heard it. The folk three miles across just may have. A smile comes over you. Geez, what a moment. My horse just formed a sentence, but nobody is going to believe me.

Both Jessie and Shanti told me, 'You can ride me now', and that is when I climbed up into the saddle. Both experiences were like a dream, with little fuss and buck and both horses still love to be ridden.

So, I waited and then she spoke.

'Yes, Bron, I would like a baby.'

I found a majestic black and white Paint stallion with a very good nature and after a couple of months in Grafton, Jessie came back to the farm with a new glow and a slightly swelling belly full of promise. The almost twelve months that followed were the equivalent of floating on a cloud of sheer delight. It was so exciting to imagine that a baby horse was forming inside my beautiful girl. We walked and talked each day and at night I sang songs to her on my guitar, while giving the reassurance that a maiden mare often needs. This was her first time to be pregnant and my first time with a planned equine pregnancy. We were working it all out together, with the help of books, vets, horse friends and faith.

Shanti was also a big part of this preparation and seemed to understand all the different needs that Jessie had emotionally. Shanti is an adorable pinto and my daughter's horse. She is also the herd leader and took it upon herself to look out for the expectant mother. The baby grew and grew and began to kick very hard anytime I placed my hand on the mother's belly. I thought without a doubt, that my Jess was having a filly. I had picked out the name, Annie Oakley. If by chance, the foal was a colt, I had chosen the name Blue Jeans. I loved this name, but I did not think that I would ever use it.

The build-up to the birth of the foal was quite considerable. Jess was ten days over her due date and having her tail bandaged each night with regular milk and vulva checks. Invasive thoughts and feelings had flown out the window. We trusted each other and everything was in place. Around this time, the weather was unusually erratic: Wild storms and heavy rain, then sun, with lightning and thunder and flooding, I moved my girl into the stables. She was already so late, so I decided it would be wise to bunk down for the night in the stall next to her.

I remember lying there and thinking, with the comforting sound of the rain on the tin roof with my horse and her baby just across the way… this is Heaven. On my rough blanket and bed of sawdust, I fell asleep, waking up three hours later and wondering if I had missed anything. She was quiet. I contemplated whether I should just go back to sleep, then thought, no, I had better go and check her. As I opened my eyes fully, I looked into the eyes of another. A red belly black snake had crept into the stall somehow and was stretched out to my right. Holy crap! I have a phobia and for a split second, considered that I was perhaps facing my most vulnerable and final moment on Earth. I shifted gears with lightning speed. Up and over the stable wall I scampered, like Spiderman in his favourite green pyjamas. I haltered my very fat, untroubled mare and led her back to the house paddock, with my bare feet sinking and sliding through the perilous mud. Storm was over.

Would the baby ever be born? It was Saturday evening and I decided to watch another birthing video.

The battery in my laptop died suddenly. It was time to go check on Jess again. As I pushed open the screen door, I saw the sac and one leg protruding from her rear end. It had started! I grabbed a torch, my phone, put on my dressing gown and I made my way to Jess, who was wondering when I would turn up and had no idea what was happening to her.

I remember feeling so overwhelmed with joy. I kept saying over and over to absolutely nobody, *I can't believe I am going to see the birth! I can't believe I am going to see it! OMG, I'm going to see it!* I was so excited. Mares are usually very secretive with birthing. It is said that they do not choose the birth date of their foals, but they choose the time and place of that date. Jess had chosen eleven p.m. on a clear country night, right by the flame tree, in a very soft and comfortable spread of grass, about a small stone's throw from my bedroom.

She was unsure of her body. Her face looked at me for understanding. I spoke gentle words to her. *It will be okay girl. You can do this. You will know how to do this.* Her contractions were powerful as she hoisted her heavy, pregnant body up and down from the ground, legs wobbling, straining to work the baby out. The foal was in the right position and while I was talking with her, I was filming with my phone. I looked over my shoulder and Tigger, our sixteen-year-old Tabby cat, was sitting primly on the neat woodpile near the paddock gate. As if overseeing events, he glanced with an acumen far beyond his human/cat years, like some celebrated senior surgeon. I was amazed at how calm and connected the farm had become to this moment in time. Everything on the land went still.

Legs were out and then a nose and then a very long hold up. An hour and he looked stuck. I began to get a sick feeling in my stomach. No, here comes his head, but his tongue was hanging out the side and he was not looking good. Jess got to her feet again and he began to disappear back inside her with a ripped sac. I put down my phone and said to my beautiful big girl, "On the ground Jess, next contraction, I am going to help." My mind was racing to a place that is hard to write about. I felt that he was already gone. I was scrambling through my thoughts, trying to cope, talking to the franticness that was now making me want to vomit. The foal has gone, Bron, you need to help your mare and get the baby out and then you need to get a shovel and bury this baby before the sun comes up. You need to honour this birth and this horse you love so much. Cowgirl up. You can think about the hard parts later. I was crying from my inside, but the tears were hidden at the back of my heart. They were sternly put on notice. *No crying. No way. Just get in there and get the baby out.*

My mare went down and began a very strong contraction. I reached into her body and found a shoulder and then an opposite side jaw. As she pushed, I pulled and out the foal slipped with a rush of blood and sticky fluid. The face moved and I realised with the purest form of joy, that this baby was warm, not cold. I tore at the sac and watched a miracle come to life in my hands; coughing, spluttering fluid from brand new lungs, eyes opening, legs moving and the smell, the immense presence of this sacred perfume. So sweet. Like honeysuckle or caramel cookies or ... I cannot make a comparison really. It was a Heavenly smell, and it was all over me and this little one.

Once the sac was off, I stroked the new horse, using soft words again. My girl was not moving. She was exhausted. I walked over to check on her. Jessie was just incredibly tired and not sure of what had happened. I patted her and told my horse she had a baby.

I wondered whether this baby was a colt or a filly, so I lifted their tiny, wet tail and discovered a little colt. But there was something else that really had my attention. He was jet black. He had a white star and four long white socks, but on his shoulders, he had tiny white wings. I checked both sides and yes there was a matching set. He had been born into the world with intricately designed wings in his paint horse markings and a tuft of white mane in this same spot, that created the image of feathers.

The foal was shivering and Jess was still not moving, so I took off my dressing gown and wrapped it around him. He was warm and alive and I could not believe my eyes. How privileged was I to be part of this special moment in time. We had time. The three of us: The horse I love, her new baby and the horse lover, me.

The night was so still and the air cooling by the hour. The stars were flickering with pride, and Tigger, unmoved by events, remained on his grandstand seat, purring softly into the night. I felt the spirit of my deceased father around. We had shared ownership of my Quarter Horse mare. I wanted to name the colt in that moment. I had a long list of suitable names but only one stuck out in my mind and in my heart.

'Dad, I want to call him Blue Jeans.'

I spoke as if I was seeking this final permission. I heard my father reply from that place within,

'Bron, that is a very good name. It is duckey do.'

I knew it was dad talking because this was the very thing that my father would say about things that were just too fantastic for words. His name was Blue Jeans. It was declared before the mountain and the stars and the heavens. Blue Jeans.

The little fella whinnied for the very first time. A deep, laughing, playful call and Jessie nickered back the love of a million lifetimes. Horses adore their young, they maintain the deepest of bonds with all other horses. They talk to each other, over paddock fences, in wild herds and especially in the very beginning stages. There was so much to say.

Jess stood up. I went to my mare and tied what was left dangling from her vulva into a firm knot. It was swaying like a tennis ball on a string and I knew that gravity could now help pull the afterbirth out of her body. Blue Jeans was scrambling to his very long and unsteady legs, repeatedly falling gently on the soft grass. No dressing gown now, he was determined to get onto the milk and mother and son gently touched skin to skin. He was a little fighter and all I could see was the most beautiful story unfolding before my heart, a gorgeous black colt and those unmistakable wings.

I did not sleep at all. Instead, I watched the sun come up and learned how a young foal starts life. He came over to me often and wanted my voice and hands to stroke his shoulders. I realised that we had probably imprinted. My plans for his birth were quite different. I was going to sit back and watch, not intrude in any way. But life had another plan. I was not his mare, but I was so connected to him and he to me. My mare was very accepting of that closeness. I made a cup of tea and just drank it and the beautiful movie before me in, as the sun rose on a brand-new life. What miracles nature has kept hidden safely away in her hope chest! There was so much love. My daughter's horse, now Aunty Shanti, adored him and came over the fence to welcome Blue Jeans into her heart. He was thrilled to find another horse with patches, just like him. In fact, I am sure I saw those very thoughts cross his curious little elfin face.

I gently moved mother and foal into my house paddock and spent the morning sending out baby announcements over text. The long-awaited appearance from the little messiah was finally here. I gave my mare time alone, although watching from a distance. She was gentle and tentative to his every need. He loved her and hid behind her flanks when something flash caught his eye. The mountain had a new baby. The farm was smiling from cheek to cheek and the sun eventually went down on a colt that had a beautiful blue sheen in his now brown baby coat. With his eyes closed and his neck tucked into his chest, he looked like a mystical seahorse. There was something so special about him. Just being around him, made you very happy inside. These are not only the words of a lovesick horsewoman who finally met her ten-year-old dream. These words were echoed time and time again, from every human being that came to visit. He got to you somehow. Like when you sing in church and the goose bumps along your arms turn into emotional firecrackers. He drew you in with his soft, liquid brown eyes and then he hit you with something.

Pure Love.

Chapter 3
The Unexpected Horror

There is a Buddhist saying that goes something like this: "For a hard person, give them lots of kindness, for a soft person, give them something very hard." The shadows had returned. Blue Jeans was limping on his far side front leg. When he was born, his back legs had been slightly bent in, but after a lengthy conversation with the vet, I was assured that in a few days this would disappear and that they would straighten out. They did.

I hoped that what I saw now, was just a hiccup but as the limping became more pronounced, my heart sank. A visit from the vet confirmed the fears. He either had an abscess, a fracture, or a break. What on earth had caused this, I could not imagine. My farm was not a perfect farm, the ground was not flat, more undulating and crooked in some places. I had done my best to keep him safe, but something had happened. How could I not see what was coming? What had I overlooked? What had I done to this baby? I wanted to throw up. I felt it was all on me. The vet asked me would I be considering euthanasia if it turned out to be more sinister? No. Not a chance. There must be a way through. I wanted to find the way through. I could not kill a foal and he was such a fighter. He had survived his birth.

Blue Jeans and Jess were moved into the stables. He was given antibiotics and bute as a painkiller and a review would be taken after the next few days, on whether an abscess had cleared up and the limping stopped. It didn't.

Giving a young horse medication is not an easy feat. I needed help with handling him and help arrived in the form of the most generous and giving horsewoman I have ever met. Cassidy turned up from a farm down the road. We hardly knew each other, but she just dived in and gave up her time and energy to assist this limping baby. The development of certain muscle groups can happen in many ways. You can lift weights, do yoga, run and stretch, but try grabbing a 100kg colt around the chest and lower rump, steady him in a steel iron grip and stay there no matter how many times he kicks up and out. This was a new twice daily workout for me, while Cass very adeptly administered his medicine via a syringe to his mouth. We could have joined the rodeo circuit. Our skills in wrestling and jamming paste into a wild bronco baby were swiftly honed.

There was no improvement, and the next step was for his leg to be x-rayed. My cowgirl friend offered to float my mare and foal to the vet's horse clinic about forty minutes down the road. I had nightmares the night before, of a foal jumping out of the float and being hit by a car on the highway. No such thing ever happened but the shadow still lurked. What was going on? I was caught in a place of tears and this thumping shock. My mare being such a steady girl, walked straight up into the carrier and I peered over at this little horse with a very sore leg, tucked in safely next to her as Cassidy drove slowly and carefully to the clinic.

I went home to a farm that now had no foal or mare and I waited for the vet's phone call. They would be staying at the clinic for three days. I tidied up the stables, talked to Shanti, my daughter's horse and genuinely felt as if my insides now dwelled permanently in my throat. What had happened to the miracle, remember, the birth, the wings, the love? What on earth was happening?

The x-rays showed a fracture and the vet had sent them off to a specialist in Coffs Harbour. She would call me back again very soon. I waited. The call came and it was now two fractures in the sesamoid bone. This bone is around the fetlock or 'ankle' of a horse. This was a serious injury. A deadly one. I asked and I asked, is there any chance of recovery? "Yes," said the vet, "There is. He can completely heal but he must be in the stable now for the next four weeks at least."

I was so relieved. There was a way through it and he had a strong spirit. I knew I could work with this and pushed all feelings of fear aside to jump into action. Cassidy stayed with me every morning and night to keep up his medicine, then my daughter arrived home from Canberra and took over that medicine call. He loved my girl and she used her magic to get him to take that medicine across the stable door, no rodeo hold was necessary. My lower back was elated! She also played peek-a-boo with him and wiggled that syringe in a way that he could not ignore. My daughter is studying to be a primary school teacher and I guess that speaks for itself. She has the patience and the inroads into little people's minds and hearts and as it turned out, that also included colts.

I read Blue Jeans stories, I thought it might break up the boredom for him. I put my daughter's horse in the stall across from them, which really helped to settle Jess. I set up swinging toys, but he grew sick of those after a couple of days. I took my guitar up at night and sang all the farm songs I could remember. My horses usually love the strum of the guitar and they all have their own song. I wrote and sang his song, *My Name is Blue Jeans* and he, like the other animals, recognised his name in amongst the tone and the story of the love we felt for him.

The nights up at the stable were so special even though this horribly hard thing had happened. I would sit and talk to our horses, play songs, then my daughter would appear with a cup of tea, and we would share stories of his little antics that day. I was aware that something bigger was taking place. Circumstances, really challenging ones, can make us change our automatic routine and view life in ways that make every single second count. He blinked and we cooed. Everything this little fella did was beautiful and amazing, even the naughty stuff.

He had kicked out a few times and one day, he just walked up and bit my arm. It really hurt but I could not stay mad for long. He was just testing his new razor-sharp teeth ... on me. He loved eating manure and rolling in it. Keeping the stables clean was hard enough, let alone keeping a foal clean. I found it difficult to watch my very dignified mare living amongst urine and manure every hour of the day, every day of the week, even though I cleaned out their stable morning and night. I watched depression hovering around her face and I felt it creep into her heart.

Every three days I moved them to the opposite stall, just ten steps across, with my ute and an old screen door propped up to create a blocked pathway, so that no foal could escape and damage his leg further. I gave them both a warm bath with a washer at the end of each day, to clean up the filth on their bodies. My mare was so grateful and Blue Jeans began to hug me around this time.

I brushed him from head to hoof and started laying his little blue halter on his head, shoulder and rump, playing a game with it, getting him used to the feeling of the future. I hugged him back with all the love I could dig from my heart. He let me put a poultice on his fetlock each day. I asked the vet if this would be okay. It was. I made up warm and cold packs for his leg, using everything from comfrey, carrots, potato, turmeric, garlic and Epsom salts. I prayed for him every morning and I waited for guidance. Today it was comfrey again and this time it was warm. The advice from spirit was so clear, that I did not once question it. He put out his leg for my hand each time I entered the stable. He really loved these poultices. They stayed on for three hours and he would lay down and rest his leg, while I brushed him and stroked his little face.

His bones were still growing, so they needed minimal binding and restriction, especially his fractured bones. My mare was on supplements to assist bone growth, that Blue Jeans was receiving via her milk. I was researching stories online and speaking to other vets, gathering as much information as I could. My own vet was supportive of anything that could help with his healing.

Every now and then I would break down crying. Not just little crying, these deep, heaving sobs. Then I would go back up to the stables to feed them and this little face would look at me over the door. He had no idea of the pain and terror I felt in my heart. He just had love to give. Love and hugs and curiosity—every time.

Chapter 4
Coming Into Full Bloom

I met my Bron when I was a yearling. In horse and human language, that means I was twelve-months-old. But I met her long before then. I was this human's old Quarter Horse, Beau. My spirit had come back again to spend more time with her. She did not know that when she found me. I remembered the time before and her father, as they had both come to look at buying a new horse, some thirty-five years ago. I stood next to them in the yard and put my head over Bron's shoulder. She had just ridden me—she was fifteen-years-old. Her father was saying,

'Oh, he's big, maybe a bit too much horse there for you, Bron.'

My coat was dappled and shining in the spring sun and my eyes had already connected with hers. I knew this was my Keeper, I just had to remind her of what already lay in our hearts. So, as I reached over those small shoulders, I locked my muzzle into her chest, and in that moment when my spirit connected with hers, she knew. Her father saw this gesture and he also knew. I was her horse and without any further hesitation he spoke the all-important words.

'We will take him!'

I did not have a privileged life in the twelve years before that time. I was used as a trotter and had developed a dislike for any kind of harnessing, restriction, shouting and roaring. On many occasions I bucked Bron off my back—nobody had taught me anything about spray jackets that squeaked or girths that could pinch. I came through the era where horses were broken in roughly and swiftly, with no time taken for desensitising or building trust with the changes we must face. But my new owner was different. She was a teenage girl who loved me. She brushed my coat and talked endlessly about silly boys at school or plans she had for travelling around and one day owning a farm. I was with her all the way. I never hurt Bron, but I challenged and frightened her many times. She just kept coming back.

One day we both looked death squarely in the eye. A huge moving road vehicle, called a semi-trailer came up the narrow road that led to my paddock. It had no right being there but there was no changing the situation. We were out on our usual ride together, no saddle and I was jammed into the wrong side of the road, with nowhere to run. The canopy around this truck was flapping wildly, in tune with the roar of its gigantic wheels and I felt every nerve in my body wanting to jump into nothing. Bron talked to me. She saw that my greatest fear was approaching. She leant down, put her hand on my neck and told me, not to be afraid, just let this monster pass. As the truck came to my side, I went down on my four legs. Her legs slid along the gravel road beneath us and in this moment, she was looking directly under the huge rattling vehicle. I stayed there and I shook and shook. It was all I could think to do. The truck passed and I got to my feet. My Keeper was shaking on my back for what seemed like forever.

'You saved us, Beau. You are such a good horse. You saved our lives.'

Personally, I think it was a joint effort, but I became her hero after that time. We never, ever forgot it and our bond grew deeper because of it.

I died and went back to Heaven when I turned twenty-eight, my Bron was thirty-one. She had retired me on a farm in Forster, NSW and drove up to see me from time to time, with carrot cake and apples and old conversations. I loved those visits and looked forward to seeing her. I deteriorated in my old age alongside the inevitable suffering that can bring an animal. My Keeper took an unexpected call amidst her busy life in the city and gave permission for a vet to help me home via a needle. I was grateful to her then—my body was hurting me. As I left the Earth, I felt my spirit fly straight through her heart. Every ride, every stroke, every moment we had shared, resounded between us. She cried so deeply and I scooped those sad, empty feelings into the pocket of my heart, knowing they were my treasures.

The *Pastures of Endless Light* are where all the horses go. I went home, my time with her was finished for now. You could think of this other home as a resting place, a healing place, but it is also incredibly social. I met up with old friends, horses I had known before Bron and horses I had met along the way. We shared our human stories. I believed I had the best of stories, because I had her. My friends would sit and listen and nod their heads,

'Oh, so good, did you really drink her beer?'

Yes, I did. I was a big part of her family. Her father even rode me on weekends and her little brother would double sometimes behind my Western saddle. I was loved.

When an angel told me, that I would go back to Bron, that we had more to share, I was simply elated. Heaven is different to Earth in that you can see what is happening to a loved person very clearly. I watched Bron fall in love, get married and have a baby. I watched her playing horses with her toddler, giving her horsey rides and the cheeky toddler wanting to be her foal. I saw the game where her daughter, lay under Bron's belly and pretended to be a sleeping baby horse, while my Bron played the role of doting mare. I loved seeing and feeling how much I was remembered in my Keeper's heart.

It seemed only natural to pay a visit to Bron's little girl in her dreams. I introduced myself one evening and started teaching her about horses and how they like to be trained. Then I sat back with my friends and watched as this daughter shared her new information with her mother, including the words:

'Beau told me this and Beau told me that. He is this big, dark horse and he says he knows you, mum, he says that you know him.'

The seed was already planted, and I felt waves of joy as Bron realised that something special was happening from an old friend she had thought she would never connect with again. I was not dead. I was getting busy.

Of course, her daughter loved horses. She had the genealogy and even though they lived a city life, she had her mother's heart around her, that carried every single horse story imaginable within it. To say she was affected would be an understatement—knowingly or unknowingly.

At eight-years-old, Leilani saved up all her Christmas and pocket money and bought her first horse, Twilight an elderly black mare. Shortly after that, her mother and father sold their beach house for a mountain farm an hour away from town. Twilight carried Leilani to the school bus stop each morning and her mother rode her back to the farm. She is a dear old friend of mine who wanted to meet my human family. She only had a few years to lend and help break in a new beginner rider before it was her time to return to Heaven. A spirited pinto called Shanti joined them shortly after, then one day, Bron's father said,

'I think we should get a Quarter Horse again, like Beau. Then you and Leilani could ride together Bron. I want to go halves in the ownership of a Quarter Horse with you.'

Yes, the seed was certainly sprouting and I had already been born back on Earth. I had already made my way to find my old Keeper again.

I was a yearling. She saw me in an online ad as I was grazing optimistically, just twenty miles down the road from where she lived. I watched from the paddock as her father and she walked onto the property. It was just like old times. I remembered this movie. They were coming to see me. My owner brought me to them in a halter, I was not broken in. My color and my white markings were almost identical to the ones I had when I was her Beau. I wondered if she would notice this because now, I was a filly, and my name was Jessie. She took one look at me and she knew, but it wasn't my outside that Bron saw, it was my heart, my spirit. I wrapped my neck around her shoulder and put my muzzle deep into her chest. She remembered. Her father was amazed and declared that he had never seen a horse more loving. Well, yes, he had. I was the same horse, now a mare, not a gelding.

I was sold to my dearest friend and our story continued. There was so much to catch up on. But it had to be done gently. I reminded her so much of someone, but she did not know why or how that could be. I wanted her to see me, to know fully in her heart that I was Beau, but I could not just drop it all on her, so I leaked this information in stages. The angels from *The Pastures* helped me. They sent her dreams that alluded to this simple fact and then when she had broken me in and was on my back, I would occasionally do little tricks from my past. I had no need to buck or fight out, my learning with Bron had been so gentle, but I would snort a certain way or change my gait suddenly. She closed her eyes when we galloped, and she knew. There was only speed, wind, manes flying, minds soaring and one spirit, not two. Jess and Beau were the same. Jess and Beau and Bron were the same.

I was eight-years-old when Bron asked me if I would like a baby. It was the most beautiful gesture and I knew that I was going to have this in my story this time. I knew I had a dear friend from Heaven that wanted to be my son and Bron's colt. Plans for his arrival were already underway in *The Pastures* and were now a part of my paddock dreams. I was being prepared for change and after all our years of riding together, I could think of nothing more beautiful than to share a baby horse with my Keeper.

A mate was chosen for me, and he was a kind and gentle stallion. I returned to Bron with my foal already forming in my rounded belly and hormones that made me both happy and sensitive. My diet was enhanced and every day I was checked and assured by my special girl, that all was well. I could feel the joy in Bron's heart. It went deeper than just the excitement of a new horse. It was her lifetime dream. I was carrying the precious daydream of a ten-year-old girl in my tummy. I was overjoyed to do this, not just as a mare but as a lifelong friend. I knew that it was some kind of miracle, how dreams and special things can come together.

Almost twelve months had passed before the first contraction. The birth was overdue but not really. There were some last-minute details being sorted out in *The Pastures of Endless Light.* When a new horse comes in, they are given an overview of their story with the humans they will meet. Sometimes, the details need a lot of discussion and preparation. The angels that look after horses really do care for finer details. They take time to share some of the story, assuring that they will be there, around the Earthly pastures, helping young and old horses to assimilate to this world and its challenges. There is always love and always spirit, it does not matter what story or what landscape we are living in. My colt needed extra time in his Heavenly pasture. He was being prepared and he was perfectly on time for his physical life when he was born.

It was planned that Bron would be at his birth and part of that beginning. I needed her there because he did not birth easily. You could say that I had a traumatic birth and that would be true, but I also had the most miraculous of births and that is how I remember it. I was unable to move, I had pushed him out and Bron had helped. He was in her arms. She was talking softly to him, assuring him, he was safe and she took off her dressing gown and wrapped it around his quivering, wet body. I looked at them and I felt love.

He called to me, I nickered back and we spoke our deepest language. He was just beautiful. Jet black and feisty and a baby. I looked at my son and I saw his wings. All the time he was inside me, he had wings.

I remembered something from Heaven, conversations I had had with other mares and the *Angels of the Light.* I remembered that there would be something different about my baby. They told me that it would be seen on the inside and on the outside. I was looking at the outside. I had given birth to a youngster with a set of white wings. The inside, I knew in the deepest parts of my equine heart. My son was an angel.

Chapter 5
Baby Blue Jeans

To introduce myself to you is to ask that you think of me as a rather knowledgeable being. Not the kind of intelligence you might measure through academic degrees or genius findings, I have a spiritual wisdom about me that has accumulated over many different experiences of learning and exchange. I was very interested in the horse girl that was being talked about by the Pasture Angels and I spent a great deal of time speaking with Beau before he left Heaven to become Jess.

I am a horse in my nature and spirit, but I am a little different. I have been created to be both human-like and horse-like. This might sound odd but there are such creations in Heaven. We communicate things, absorb things, do things for the benefit of others, offer healing and generally we share lessons of love with both horses and people. I am celestial in my nature, which means I spend a lot of my time in Heaven in celebration of creation and communication with the One who made us all. He is a good, good soul. He is our Caretaker. So, you see, I serve and my main purpose in my life is to do just that. I work for the ultimate herd leader.

I wanted to be Blue Jeans. That is not my name really. My name is Elijah. The name that Bron chose for me, Blue Jeans, was inspired. I rather liked the sound of Elijah Blue Jeans which is now my full Heavenly name.

Bron was drawn to the name Blue Jeans through a Miley Cyrus film and an Old Cowboy Horse Names list that appeared one day on her laptop screen. We can do things like that, a little fun for a fellow who is in awe of the wishes in a ten-year-old's heart. I remember that girl who sat on the craggly branch of her front yard tree in her faded blue jeans and raggedy T-shirt. She was dreaming big and so I thought it rather fitting, to take something from that image. *Elijah Blue Jeans* represents the moment in time when we aligned ... when divinity decided. She lives in my heart, my name and my spirit. And there were other clever things I did before I met her in person.

I directed the young horse-loving Bron, to a novelty shop in Port Macquarie, a coastal town in New South Wales. She was on holiday with her family and I guided her into this shop and to a particular shelf that had a little black china colt for sale. It cost her all of her pocket money, but she wanted it so much. The china colt's mane was flowing in the wind and his legs were splayed in a frozen canter. She carried that precious ornament with her everywhere. It represented her dream; it was such a treasure to her. Then I knocked the china colt over a few times and its offside front leg snapped at the fetlock. Each time this happened, Bron would sticky tape it back on. There it was standing back on her bedroom shelf, not perfect, but still upright, until one day a thing called superglue came onto the scene and made an even better job at repair. This filled her heart with joy and even though the ornament looked fixed, there was an obvious and lasting crack.

When my fracture became visible to Bron, two weeks after I was born onto her farm, all that she could think about was her little china colt.

I am an Angel and we do things like this. We plant signs and messages everywhere. Not to hurt people but to help people. I knew my full story as a real life, Earth colt. I knew that it was going to deeply hurt Bron. So I prepared her and when she recalled the little china horse she tried so desperately to put back together, she felt a level of peace and she was very determined to find the superglue for me.

An Angel's heart has maximum love; A tank of overflowing energy that can knock a person out. Every time I was around my Keeper, I flipped the lid on my tank. I also did this around a few farm visitors and chuckled through the night at the comments made on how much they loved me—they hardly knew me! But they just felt something. Angels bring the essence of Heaven down with them and people and places remember the feeling of Heaven.

I did not want to waste one single moment on Earth. I had great work to do and I knew that I would also feel pain. I had two fractured bones in my leg and all I wanted to do was run. Bron moved my mother and I into her stables and I was not going to move at all for the next four weeks, except to play snow angels in the new bedding she provided every three days, or walk gently across to the cleaner stall, while the old stall was mucked out. I watched her. She worked hard to keep us clean. Then she disappeared for eight hours to another job, returning to work hard again to keep us clean once more and my mother fed. She brought her guitar up to the stalls at night and sang her country songs which included a song about me. I loved her so much. I started to communicate with Bron through the day when she was away and she heard me talking to her in her heart. She would come back to the stable and say,

'Blue Jeans, were you chatting with me today? I felt you.'

Of course I was. I wanted her to realise something more about me.

Bron was also treating my fracture. She would pray in the mornings and the *Angels from The Pastures of Light* would tell her exactly what to put in her homemade poultices. They were warm and comforting. I would hold my leg out for her and wait patiently while she wrapped them into the bone. I hugged her every morning and many times through the day. My hugs were not just physical. I would place my neck up and over her shoulder and turn my muzzle into the centre of the top of her spine. Then I would shoot love all through her. She would respond via her heart. It poured all that she had inside into my little horse chest. Our hugs could last for more than a few minutes. She loved me and I loved her.

I was not what Bron expected. I had a very serious fracture, two in fact. I required round the clock care. I listened at night as this human cried herself to sleep with fear. She felt responsible for my situation, but she was not responsible. She was helpless in it, but she was not the helpless type. She feared that I would die, but I was alive. She wanted the story to be different, but it could not possibly be, it was the story our Creator decided upon. She feared that all the love she felt in her heart would be taken from her, but how could it ever be? For nothing that is loved so deeply can ever disappear. I had to teach her that love was never-ending. I had to show her that we must keep believing and trying and I had to love her and love her, because Bron already had another kind of broken part, long before I came to be her colt.

My name is Elijah Blue Jeans and I had a job to do. I came to Earth with my toolbox for a woman who needed fixing, not the cherished china colt. A beautiful woman with a fracture in her heart. I was sent by The Caretaker. I came under His direction and I was born by a woodpile with a leg that was already compromised and exactly what our story required.

You know pain of the physical kind is nothing compared to the pain that echoes through the ethers of a broken, broken soul. Sometimes you must dig deep into a wound, tear it open again and again, before the real healing can begin.

There is nothing so moving to Angels, as the desperate cry for help that comes from humans that love their horse or any animal for that matter, or any child or friend or family member. There is nothing that turns the heart of God more.

My friends gathered around Bron now. She could not see them. They all came from *The Pastures*. They knew the hard part of the story was ablaze in her heart. They wanted to comfort her and tell her that Blue Jeans was fine. He would be okay, not to worry. They turned up, just like I knew they would. Just like we had planned before I was born to her mare.

The only way to get through deep sadness and brokenness is to feel *the terrible* and to let Heaven in. Bron was praying for my leg every single day, but we were praying for her. *The Angels from The Pastures* knew a girl that needed a little bit of help.

PART 2

Chapter 6
Running the Gauntlet

Blue Jeans and Jess had spent four weeks in a stable. That may not sound like much but to a horse who usually walks endless miles grazing in a paddock, it felt like an eternity. Jessie hung her head low with eyes that could not conceal her confusion and slide into sadness. My horse has a deep trust in me and what was I doing to her? She looked at me pleading for change and I kept her locked up with her little lame baby. As a human being who loves animals and in particular horses, this was perhaps one of the hardest things I have ever done—face my horse each morning, as if everything was okay. Tell her things will be right again, but not knowing that for sure and keeping both animals locked up when all they wanted was to be horses—free and moving around. I have always talked very directly to any animal on our farm. Whenever I felt the tug at my heart, I knew that Jess was trying to talk with me.

"What is going on Bron? Why are we still in this stable? You never do this. My body is aching." I would tell Jessie that something had happened to her baby. That he needed rest in order to fix it, that is why I was doing this. I promised her, I would do everything I could to make this time comfortable for her and the foal. I did my best.

Then the best was just not going to be enough. The little fella was growing, despite the elephant in the stall and his increased height, was an equally amplified curiosity for what lay outside the stable walls. He had figured out that he could put both front legs up onto an internal shelf and was considering how to hoist himself off the ground, over the wall and smack onto the grass outside with his little glass leg. He showed me his intentions one afternoon, when I flew home from work with a weird feeling in my stomach. He was talking to me on the inside again and I knew he was about to tempt fate.

If he launched from his now quite powerful Quarter Horse rear end, he could scramble over the height of the stable wall and smash that tender fetlock to pieces. I was frozen in horror and confusion. What would I do now? The stables had suddenly become a ticking time bomb for him. I had the round yard, but it was about sixty meters down the driveway. My driveway was a nightmare to navigate, even for a well-developed four-wheel drive. He could easily go down one of the several holes that had taken up residence over many years of rain and drought. I had nowhere else to put him.

This thing began that I can only describe as terrifying, spontaneous, triage. I had to make one decision based on where the greatest disaster lie and chose the slightly lesser very real danger zone. It made me want to vomit. Was I hammering a nail in his coffin? But I could not leave him in the stable any longer. I was so grateful that he had communicated to me, what he might do. What would happen when I went to sleep for the night? I had to move them now.

The day was going to turn to night within half an hour. I tried to ring my vet to confirm the decision I had made. Four weeks had passed, his leg was looking good, and he was strong on it. Surely, this was the next step for his recovery—move him out of a place that he had now outgrown and somehow outsmarted.

I could not get hold of the vet, so I rang my mother, the one human being who has always helped me over the years with unpacking and resolving impossibly hard predicaments. My mum could not give me the correct horse safety answer but asked that all-important, *what is your gut telling you* question. My gut said, I had to move them, even though the risk of injury was also extremely high. *Then move them.*

I strapped up his injured bones and put an extra foam boot around them. I talked to my mare and told her what was happening and how I needed her to walk extra slowly with me down the hill to the round yard. She listened. As we made our way out of the stable, I looked back a couple of times to see a happy little colt staying closely by his mother. She must have given him a strict talking to. That sparky little fella must have wanted to run. He was finally free of the four stable walls, but he did not move beyond the slow pace we were taking. The round yard felt like it was days away and we had set out on some great trek across the desert. We approached all the nasty holes in the road, but both horses stepped over and around them. I was starting to breathe again—we were almost there. I walked them in through the front gate and released the halter and lead rope from my Jess. Her heart lifted like a warm sponge cake. I felt all the heaviness within her, depart through doorways of sheer delight as she began grazing at the lush grass the yard provided. Her baby copied her, pretending to know all about grazing as I closed the steel gate to seal them in. I cried tears of joy and absolute thankfulness for the simple fact that nobody had been hurt walking sixty meters across my farm.

I leant comfortably against the yard rails and stayed well into the darkness, just watching my horses be horses. After I took off his bandages, Blue Jeans suckled for a while then lay amongst the long threads of green grass. One of his wings could be seen in between the blades. I took a snapshot in my mind and on my phone. There was an Angel in the round yard and this peace came over the mountain that I cannot really describe. All the anguish and turmoil of his beginnings were now filled with renewed hope. He was so happy. She was so happy. I was so happy. Life was becoming normal again. Hanging out with horses was normal—not fearful, not cruel, not deadly.

But the gauntlet is relentless. Just when you think you have conquered one challenge, the next is always waiting for you and it does not allow the breath to settle into its favourite rhythm for too long.

It was now the middle of summer and my long teacher school holidays were so perfectly timed. I had completed all next year's lesson plans so I had zero teacher paperwork to do. Every minute of my day was focused on his healing and being amongst my beautiful herd. Shanti had joined us down in the new location and could talk to both mare and foal more freely over the round yard rails, from the adjacent paddock she was now grazing in.

Blue Jeans loved his Aunty. She adored him and would nibble at his mane, cleaning him as if he was her own child. I was privileged to watch them all in their daily routine and witness the deeper bonds that horses share—the ones we often miss while they are out grazing in paddocks, waiting for their next ride. In a way, I got to live with them. In a way, they got to live with me. My dirty denim overalls really reeked of manure, urine, sweat and dirt. I spent many hours on the ground with him, resting his head on my lap, while I sang songs and read more stories. The bottom of the round yard was bedded out like the bottom of a well-worn cattle yard. All grass was gone, just clay and horse shit now. I cleaned it morning and night, shovelling droppings steadily into my wheelbarrow, but the smell lingered on, and the grime just became part of the equation for each special day in equine company.

In the morning he would call to me with the other horses. Each mare would whinny a greeting then Blue Jeans would add his little number. It was a combination of cheek, joy and then a bit of deep resounding testosterone thrown in. He had the most beautiful voice. It pierced my heart every time he greeted me. He had learnt that this is how you talk to a human. You say gidday.

He was also fascinated with my ute, Henry. Each time I drove up the driveway and passed the round yard, Blue Jeans would move to the side and stare at my Hylux, like some infatuated kid. I could read his thoughts: *Wow, what a vehicle. What is she doing in that thing? How it moves.* He was captivated by Henry and as I made my way to him, I would wind down the window and sing out,

"Hallo little fella, do you like my old truck?"

The bad weather had set in and turned the floor of the yard to quicksand. As I drove home one afternoon, I looked for my colt and found him lying on his side in the pouring rain. I had made a little shelter out of a shade sail, and he would get under it with his mare, but as I was chugging up the driveway in my powerful Hylux, my heart bottomed out. He was not moving.

Racing to his side, I established that he was breathing and warm, but it did not make sense that he was laying the way that he was. I checked all his legs, they were fine, even the leg that was healing looked as it had from the morning. Then I noticed something on his back and could not believe what I saw ... a gaping hole of raw and torn flesh. Then as if to highlight this picture further, he lifted his head and bit at the hole, making it deeper and bloodier. It was the size of a small football. I stared at it and I shook. My mind was just scrambling, screaming, scraping at any ideas that could make sense of how it should now be on this foal's body. Why was he suddenly so gruesomely distorted?

In all my years of fixing cuts and rips and tears on horses, I had never seen anything as gory as this ... on a baby. Why? Why? Why? Then, I have to fix this! I have to help him! I looked back at his face and even though it was now raining hard, I could see these tears coming out of his eyes. They became my tears. I sat down in the mud and the rain for one moment and I cried hard with him. So hard that I believe both our hearts melded and he knew that I could feel his pain. I wondered, could he feel mine?

My heart had snapped open with the deepest shock and sadness, then snapped straight into action. I ran for everything medical I owned that could possibly help a wound. I rang my cowgirl friend, Cassidy, who was at the round yard in a blink with everything medically connected to horses she owned, and we pooled our resources and our experience to help this gaping disaster before us, to heal.

It was so tender and inflamed. He did not want his back touched and kept on aggravating things by biting at it. Something must have irritated him. There were bugs and mosquitoes and all the lovely things that Summer brings, stirred in a cocktail of mud, manure and urine. It seemed that the contents of Mother Nature were really stacked against this little guy. He wasn't safe anywhere!

I cleaned the wound with a wash, but it had nowhere to run, so I mopped up any liquid with a clean towel that I had to throw on his back quickly, pat down, then retrieve from the ground as he tore it off. His now increased ingestion of bute assisted him with pain and antibiotics were also given internally. I found it hard to look at the wound for too long. I knew I had to get in there and heal it, but it was a ghastly view ... that overhead shot of a hole in the back of a six-week-old baby.

What was amazing was, this had drawn attention away from his leg, even though both areas were being treated. I still made his poultices, but I went to sleep crying about his back, not his leg. Nothing was working to heal it. I mean nothing. Even some of the higher range medical products did not come through for him. Behind the scenes Cass had written to a horse friend who made all natural products for wounds on horses. She had sent away for an ointment known as Babe's Gold and presented it one morning at the round yard as an early Xmas present. What a kind and thoughtful thing to do.

The minute this cream went onto the little colt's back, he stopped tearing at the hole. Getting the cream on, required calling him over to the open steel gate, one girl brushing his face (Cassidy), the other smearing the cream on the hole while he wasn't looking. He had become so protective and sensitive to anyone or anything being anywhere near his back. It was so hard to see and feel all that built up trust now broken. He took one hundred steps back from where we had been. He just would not let me touch him.

But we tricked him and when I went to check the next morning, the wound had sealed, it was clean, and it had even shrunk in size. It was another miracle! His eyes were bright, he was up and suckling and couldn't care less about his back. Within the next few days and an application of this natural cream morning and night, the wound was disappearing from the picture. Blue Jeans was once again in a very good space. His leg was strong, his back was healing, tick, tick. Things were coming back to normal, or perhaps the new normal. Not sure.

He stood away from me one morning as I was cleaning up the yard. Blue Jeans would often follow me around as I picked up the manure with my shovel. He would dip his nose into the small of my back and let me know that he was right behind me. I would talk to him and tell him,

"Hey, now it's a hotel in here little fella, so much cleaner."

He would then walk me to the gate as I emptied out the fill into a portion of the paddock that now held my budding ideas for a new garden.

But not this morning, this one morning, he stood away from me. I looked up at him and he was standing straight and strong on all four legs. There was no evidence of any weakness, injury, or distortion. His head was high, his nostrils slightly flared, his eyes dazzling like distant stars. I saw his wings, his new jet-black coat emerging through his ruffled brown baby fur, and his spirit so proud and strong. He was a Quarter Horse. I had a brand-new Quarter Horse on my farm. He showed me how he would look when he was solid and grown. He looked like this. Amazing. Powerful. A fighter. Victorious. He was without a doubt, the most beautiful horse I have ever seen. It was ever so brief, a glimpse, a clearly defined moment in time. There it was. The truth about Blue Jeans.

Chapter 7
Surrendering

When my son stood up after birth, there was something different. One of his front legs was not straight and strong, and his back legs were curved under, he struggled to stay on them for too long. I felt this more than it could be seen, because even to the trained eye, his challenge and difference were very subtle at that early stage. But I knew. I remembered the important messages I had been given in Heaven. You will have a foal one day and there will be some very big impediments. Your Keeper will take care of you both, so follow her lead and surrender to her care. We were now in a stable and not able to move around naturally in a paddock. I was following her care, even though I did not like it very much at all.

My baby did not fuss, he played with his swinging toy that hung from the stable rafter, suckled for his meals, and slept on the warm, dry sawdust. I watched as he built a bond with my Bron. He looked forward to hearing her footsteps approaching at different times through the day and night. For him it meant a cuddle, a kind word, a brush and at least once a day, a nice warm poultice. As the days drew on, I stared listlessly into the soul of my Keeper and tried desperately to communicate with her.

"Why are we here? Can't we at least go out for a little while?" She heard my voice and assured me that our time would not be too long, explaining that there was a reason. Blue Jeans had fractured two bones in one of his front legs. He had to be kept still and I had to be with him to feed him. I understood and I surrendered once more to the fate that lay before me.

My body was grimy and smelled of urine and manure. My mane was dry and lifeless like thirsty wheat in a drought. My legs ached from bearing the weight of my post-pregnancy body, overflowing udders and constant standing while my baby had his milk.

Shanti had been placed in the stall opposite me and selflessly broke the silence and melancholy I felt building inside. She talked to my boy as well and taught him things like, remember to listen to mares, we are the guardians of the paddock and I am your herd leader. He looked up to her. My dear friend was so kind and patient with him. He wanted to be the leader, after all he was the colt. That would not be happening. Shanti was an Alpha mare. She had saved the herd from fire only a few years ago and so I told my son the story.

Our Bron was not on the farm. All the animals were trapped within the boundaries of the property. The firefighters had made it in time to open the back gate. Shanti had galloped us to the highest peak of the mountain, where the fire had not taken hold. Back then we had a little friend called Mudcake. She was a miniature pony Bron and her daughter had rescued. Her back legs were crippled and she was very, very old. The year before, Mudcake had given birth to a stillborn foal. Bron had called the cold little baby Thumbelina and wrapped her in her grandmother's lilac-crocheted rug. She was buried just down from the stables. It was a very sad day indeed and there were tears in the eyes of our Keeper for a long time. But mares know how to accept things. We were born this way. Survive, survive, survive. Crying cannot bring a baby back, it serves for a time, let out your sadness but you must eat, thrive and you must graze on. That is what our dear friend Mudcake did, and on that dreadful night of the fires, many of our horse friends perished. We did not, because human help came and your Aunty Shanti led us to safety. Shanti ran back down the mountain and dropped her head in the chest of one of those firefighters. She remembered the importance of saying thank you. We were so grateful. Her bravery and her unusual gesture made the pages of a country newspaper.

"So Blue Jeans, we are a herd and Shanti is our herd leader." My son now understood as he digested in thrill and wonderment more stories of bravery about the wiry paint mare across the barn.

"Oh, and one more thing my little colt, Bron calls your Aunty a unicorn. She believes this through and through and that Shanti has an invisible horn."

Now he was really listening.

I knew my son was different. So different. He was like a little child, full of wonder and curiosity but there was also something much deeper within him. Sometimes I would feel like I was in the presence of an old, old person. I was not sure if he was a horse person or a human person. He seemed to say things that horses just would not bother with. He was curious about how everything worked, especially Bron's ute. He wanted to know so many things like his life depended upon it, but when he got tired of questioning, he would huddle in beside my flank and I would love the feeling of my baby close by me, skin to skin.

I would feel his heartbeat like the tapping of a tiny fairy wren in early Spring. He was part of my body, not separate from me. Sometimes my boy would lie fast asleep under my front legs, completely trusting the 600kg weight hovering above him. I would glance at his perfect little face. His eyes were large like mine, with long lashes that closed over in sleep like soft, feathered curtains. His true coat of jet black was pushing through the fading sorrel bay. He had a big white star that looked like a smudged four-leaf clover, as it favoured one side of his forehead more than the other, a tiny white snip around his muzzle and a tuft of mane between the most expressive little ears, forever twiddling and twitching. I loved his face.

Bron was giving us a bath with a warm towel, and I thanked her as she glided gently over my legs and rump. Blue Jeans was watching, mesmerized at the union my Keeper and I shared. He knew that he could trust her because I trusted her. He knew that Bron was my dearest friend. He tried to push between us, to get his turn. He liked the feeling of that warm washer and how nice you felt after all the grime was taken away. Bron would sing to us as she cleaned us and I know my son really liked the feeling of a voice singing. The tone would hover deep into your soul and make your eyes close. When we closed our eyes, we could be somewhere else.

And then, quite magically and precipitously, we were going somewhere else. My Keeper always told me when something was about to change. We were moving to the round yard, and I was told, I had to walk very slowly to keep my son's leg safe. I understood.

I wanted to run and kick out with joy, but I followed the lead of our true alpha mare, Bron. I tip-toed down the rickety, hole-ridden driveway and steadily into the yard. There was an abundance of grass to graze on and my colt had done what I asked him to do. He did not compromise his leg. Blue Jeans was playing snow angels once more, now in the long green strips before him. He was so happy and I could not contain my joy. No more stable, just fresh air, rich green fodder, and the most glorious view off the mountain. I knew I could trust my Keeper. I knew this again and again.

But then within a couple of days, I fell once more into a mother mare's deep despair. My baby had a hole in his back, one that he was creating. He was lying in the mud in the pouring rain and in so much pain. His mid back was torn open, bloody, fleshy, raw and throbbing.

He was crying, Bron was crying, and I felt my heart drop to places I had never known before. I was going to lose him. He wasn't moving. He was sinking.

It was a long, long night and much later, I heard my Keeper crying in her own bed, I felt her praying for him, as I stood by my son.

Once more, there came a miracle for my boy. He got up and suckled by morning and Bron was working on that back. I trusted her and I told him, no matter how much it hurts, you go to her and let her help. Well, he half listened with the wise part of his soul. The other part, the little baby boy, would not let anyone near his open wound.

Eventually it healed. Some three weeks had passed, and a special natural cream had made a huge impact. It was a long time for him to be in discomfort and pain. Bron was also giving him a thing called bute once more. Not just for his leg now but for his back and another white paste for infection. He did not want any of it. I watched as my Keeper came up with ingenious ways to trick him into taking his medicine. She would wait for Blue Jeans to suckle then sprout the paste into his mouth from under my belly on the opposite side of my flanks. He fell for it every time. I would shuffle him into my teats with my muzzle and my tail, whenever I saw Bron approaching the round yard with that syringe. I could help her with this, and so I did.

At the end of the day, he would lie on the ground with his head on Bron's lap. The syringe was hidden in the back pocket of her jeans. She would sing to him and stroke his beautiful eyelids. I would love those moments together. I could have a rest from Blue Jeans and enjoy the feeling of dusk creeping over our precious mountain like a natural, numbing meditation. As the day completed itself, the clouds stopped moving, and heartbeats dropped a beat or two, then she would sing a song about being somewhere over a rainbow.

My son would begin snoring, his eyes closing ... and Bron would reach behind for the medicine she had hidden in her back pocket and shoot that paste up quickly behind his tongue, while launching into the very next verse. For just a moment, my colt would realize what had happened, then he would choose the sleep and the song over the slightest disapproval or resistance. These were the best nights I remember. She stayed with us a long time. The moon would light up the grubby old yard, its silver stream of secret promises filling us with hope and grace.

Blue Jeans was getting better.

My baby was getting better.

Chapter 8
This is Living

I wanted to talk to her. She could hear me now and then, just faintly, like a murmur amongst her deepest thinking. My Keeper needed to hear these things—the things that I brought down with me. I waited until she was asleep in her warm bed, then I began the conversation that had been specifically designed for her from *The Pastures.* She was listening, she was dreaming, yet she was awake in her soul and receptive.

Let me tell you more of where I came from. You see a foal. You see a living thing of flesh and bone that is on the Earth, flourishing in your world no matter how many challenges come along, but there is so much more to my picture. We all have a bigger picture. You, your friends, your family, the people you have not met yet, but a horse's picture looks like this:

When I am with you, I live in two worlds. My spirit is always connected to Heaven. And we have guardians or loving spirit friends that would support and guide our way. A horse is very, very sensitive and so they are often communicating back and forward from Earth to Heaven on matters to do with their life. Your mare does this, my beautiful mother, your Shanti and all the horses you have ever loved Bron, knew why they came to share a story with you and often conferred on the details of their time, with spirit messengers. You say, every single horse you loved, taught you something. Well, yes, they did. They made sure they did. These important lessons were hand crafted by a specialist group.

Before a foal is born, their spirit undergoes a briefing on their distinctive role with their chosen human. Oh yes, you were chosen Bron, just like all the others. Horses want to get close to humans and humans strive to understand their horses. From the Heavenly Pastures, we can see the people on Earth that we are most drawn to. What can we offer? What can we learn?

All these exchanges take place over time and with every single connection, love is the common link. Love is what attracts a horse to a human, or lack of love. We are noble creatures and apart from experiencing power and freedom in our majestic bodies, we only wish to serve.

I chose you Bron. I am your foal and that bond lasts for an eternity. We have long meetings in Heaven, something like an Equine Angel Council, as to whether this choice can be of benefit to not only ourselves and the human being involved, but the whole celestial herd and all creation. We are constantly communicating telepathically with each other. Love means this and love means that, so that our souls can progressively develop into a higher realm.

I mentioned that I was half horse and half human. That is the nature of my soul. I am a horse that has been emerging for some time. You could say, I have been at an intensely progressive university. I keep making observations about human behaviours. Because of this accumulated knowledge, I can affect the whole Heavenly herd in new and interesting ways. But each way offers a new window to understanding, His love— the greatest love of all, that comes from our Caretaker and is shared amongst all souls. We are His children. I belong to something much greater than my own individual self. We are all part of something much greater.

On Earth there is this illusion of separation. Human beings live apart from their Heavenly knowledge most of the time. They can recall bits and pieces of home or of Him, but they cannot quite get to know their whole bigger picture. That is where we come in Bron. We come to you, to help jolt your memory a little. We take you to those deeper places, so that you can start to remember things. Just as we have Earthly plans, so do you, so do other humans. Sometimes those plans get lost or faded along the way and a friendly reminder can come straight from the presence and customised gestures of a chosen horse.

We are creatures very dear to God. I have heard you say that you believe that was The Caretaker's best day in the office, the day he created the horse. That makes our chests fill with pride and joy Bron, to hear those words. We know we were created for a very special purpose. The love that can be felt in a little girl or boy's heart over a horse, is something quite precious both in Heaven and on Earth.

I have many friends in Heaven. My favorite hangout is a paddock by a field of sunflowers. I want to take you there Bron, just for a moment. You see several horses now, not just your foal Blue Jeans. There is an Appaloosa called Frederick, a bay pony, Jiminy Cricket, a black thoroughbred by the name of Elleena and my dear friend Poncho Toto, a striking palamino. There are horse Angels amongst us. Let me introduce you to Ezrael, Michaela, Gabriella ….

We work together to make good choices for all kinds of people. Horse people and human people. I was with these dear friends of mine when I first saw you. From Heaven, there is constant viewing of the Earthly life. You could imagine it like a huge LED monitor that runs all day and night. We are drawn to an etheric, energized screen by these little darts of love that reach into our hearts. When something is happening on Earth that is moving or interesting, you will see all rumps in the paddock swing around to observe and digest a new story.

I first saw you in this way Bron. I saw you as a little horse girl sitting in your gum tree, dreaming away. I saw the day when your Quarter Horse Beau was diagnosed with Navicular Disease and I caught the tears of a 17-year-old teenager, as she prayed desperately for some kind of miracle to save her horse. I watched as our Creator spoke to you for the very first time in your life in a way so clearly, that you could never quite shake His presence from your mind again. Your Beau was going to be put down, with his seriously lame leg, but The Caretaker told you in your plea for help, 'that everything was known, to go back to bed now, in the morning you will receive a phone call, do not worry.' You were shaken to the core. You loved that horse so much and now somebody else you had never really thought that you could believe in, was talking with you. In the morning, the phone rang and one of the most experienced equine vets in Sydney offered to use an experimental drug on Beau that would either kill him or cure him.

You chose the drug, not the bullet of a friend who had offered to put your horse down. His lameness was healed and you galloped him on that leg three years later along a beach in Port Macquarie. I was there with you Bron, even though I was living in Heaven. I wanted to be your foal and Beau, who came home to us and shared his stories, then chose to be your new filly Jessie, who is my dear mother. Now this can seem like a lot of choices, but really Bron, there is only ever one choice. We chose to respond to love.

I want you to look deeper. I want you to understand. All that you are writing is because there is something more for you to know. All the challenges we went through Bron, my birth, my fractured bones, my horrendous back wound, were all chosen experiences we needed to have—you and me and the herd and the human tribe around you. All because of important lessons in love. What you gave to me in every single moment cannot be so accurately conveyed.

I felt you grasping at the deepest fibres of your soul, like an ensnared dove, with no hope of reprieve. I witnessed the shift in your spirit when you were scurrying up and down a mountain, trying to find the right medicine to cure my latest ailment. There was a repeated experience you had, where in little bursts, you actually felt that you were a horse. You *were* becoming a horse Bron, you were in sync with us so completely and we let you ever so closely into our world. But do not forget, we also came closer to your soul and your world. I love being stroked by the resonance of the love in your voice. I love the warmth of your mountain home.

This is Living, Bron.

The very worst can be happening but kindness and nurturing and caring make the most testing of shadows fade away. This is the hope of Heaven. From my favourite pasture with my dearest friends, my story was already being fulfilled by the choices I made for the time I was going to spend with you. At ten-years- old, you dreamed of me. At one thousand, five hundred and twenty-three years old, I came to you. I heard you. I answered your call.

You saw my Heavenly home one day. You have not been able to forget that moment and have even bravely shared this experience with a few close horse friends. It was five years ago and six months on from the Pappinbarra fires. Your horses had fled the fire safely and been grazing in the paddock of your kindest neighbours, the Hensons, while you went about rebuilding the structure of your farm. When all the clearing was finished, new grass planted and growing and fences reinstated, you walked your horses back home. It was an emotional day, topped off by a gentle sprinkle of rain. You sat on your wooden fence rail and watched them all grazing under the beauty of an unexpected rainbow. Your heart was full of love and gratitude. Life was settled once more and the fire had somehow made your property more beautiful and plentiful than before, where horses and grazing were concerned.

Then it happened. Even though you were sitting on a rail, gazing down at your horses, you were suddenly taken Home and now gazing into a valley of endless light. You saw *The Pastures*. You saw hundreds and hundreds of horses standing in this Heavenly place. You saw Angels dressed in flowing white robes walking amongst these horses. They were harmonizing, something like singing, but all these different tones, and horses were bowing down to these Angels, then lying down on the ground as they were stroked and healed. The emerald-green grass, a colour you cannot really call emerald, a colour you had never quite seen on Earth and the mountains around this sacred valley that offered shelter, made a deep impression on you. Some Angels glanced back at you, they knew that you would be visiting in that brief moment in time and communicated a welcome into your heart.

You studied the faces of the horses closely. They were at peace and they were so happy to be home. You ventured into the souls of some of these horses and they all had stories to share. Some had been mistreated on Earth, some had several owners, some had been malnourished, some had been injured, some had just grown old. For a moment you glimpsed the contents of their heart. Every single horse was in a trance. They were resting in some kind of holy paddock and each Angel knew exactly what each horse needed. What sound, what tone, where to place their hands, where to move to next.

You were mesmerized and so deeply moved. When the vision left you, there were tears pouring down your face and it took all your strength not to fall off the wooden rail you were so serendipitously planted on. You knew in every aspect of your being that you had just been to Horse Heaven ... just for a moment, and in that moment, you knew something even deeper. You knew that you wanted to be that person. The one that helps them.

And so Bron, here I am. A foal that needs your help.

PART 3

Chapter 9
Equinology

It was the best summer I can ever remember on our farm. Despite all the challenges we had faced with this little horse, every day was filled with the most exquisite love. I began building small hospital paddocks for him, just across from the round yard and when he was all bandaged up with a nice cool poultice, I would walk my mare and her baby slowly into a small grassy haven. He loved this and I spent hours watching them together, enjoying life in the green, not the dirt or mud. His little racoon-colored tail would flick away tirelessly at any fly that dared to hover and every now and then, he would lift his lazy head up to take in the view. He rested, learned to graze with his mother, and wore a smile on that muzzle that could be felt in every little puff of fresh country air. I would walk them over at around three p.m. then back to the round yard on dusk. Just like the stables, it was only a few steps across. I would check his leg in the evening, and it was going strong.

On the very hot days, I faced another run with the gauntlet. The heat was unbearable in a small yard. I hosed both horses down with cool water around ten a.m.

then walked them slowly to a paddock close by that had trees for shade. It was hard to make this call because I was asking more of his leg, even though it was strapped up. He wanted to run, but he knew the rules and resisted when I spoke the words, 'slowly now'. My Jess was so happy on these days. For her, it felt like Heaven. Blue Jeans would suckle then go and lie under the mango tree. I would lose sight of him in the long green grass, but every now then, a little swish of black and white would reveal his presence. It gave me great joy in my heart to see him stretched out in a cool spot and taking in the afternoon. I watched closely as a mother would watch a child around a swimming pool. He stayed safely away from anything that could snap his leg or reopen the wound on his back. He was healing. It was very, very hot, but he was healing.

    I built a second paddock, next to the first tiny one I had made. This one was a little longer in length. I had the idea to make these rehabilitation spaces for him, that would gradually allow Blue Jeans to graze on the open mountain. The third paddock was going to be slightly sloped and moving up towards the house. In the heat and the rain and the dusty dry air, construction was taking place while curious eyes watched from the safety of their mother's side. I enjoyed giving to a horse in this way. I guess in my mind, horses have always been gold. I thought about the horses I had rescued in the past and felt grateful somewhere that my foal was giving me this kind of lesson again, despite all the horror. He was making me do things I had not done in a while. I had the urge to help another horse one day soon, and another horse. Perhaps when this little fella was through his gauntlet, I could use these paddocks for someone else in need.

There was an automatic correction in my soul, and it came from being around him. Never waste a minute on Earth. Do what you can to help. Horses are the best.

My beautiful colt was now eleven weeks old. He was strikingly handsome and had grown hopelessly cheeky and thoughtful. He hugged me every single day, every time I walked into the yard. We had a great routine. Morning was a hallo, breakfast for mum, clean the yard and horse time. Lunch was moving gently to the tiny paddock time. Late afternoons and evenings were dinner for mum, check your water again, clean your yard again, check your leg and back, then training time.

I only spent half an hour with him this way each afternoon, but he soon learned to accept the halter. I began teaching him by placing it all over his body and especially when he was laying down for a story. I put it on for the first time, this way. It did not bother him at all. Then we moved up to standing and he learned to drop his head for me slightly and accept the little blue thing on his face, around his fluffy ears and under his throat. I would brush him from head to hoof first, so he associated accepting a halter with receiving a thorough grooming session and a complimentary back scratch. I never used force. If he did not want it, I let it go, tried the next day.

He would put his injured leg up for me, directly into my hands. I held it gently, thanked him, then did some reiki on it. He did this when he was laying down as well. I also used an icepack on his fetlock while I massaged his shoulder gently, this gave him relief from any strain through the day. But all of sudden he was handing me his opposite front leg and I noticed that it was starting to bend ever so slightly out of shape. It had been taking up all the body weight since he began limping, so now I was treating both his front legs with as much alternative care and comfort that I could give.

I wanted to read *Black Beauty* to him. He was growing and he needed a growing up story. We had breezed through *The Little Mermaid*, *The Tin Soldier* and *The Ugly Duckling*, but I couldn't find my copy. I began searching on-line and had mentioned to a good friend of mine, that this was the next story I would read him. By the weekend, I had the book in my hands. Julie had gone onto Facebook and asked for a loan of *Black Beauty* for a little colt in need of a story. A lovely teacher friend had offered her copy. I was so excited and the morning was spent getting some much needed photos taken with my dear little buddy. Jules has a gift with photography and managed to capture the love that existed between Blue Jeans and myself in the most amazing snapshot—a hug that just seemed to keep on hugging. Blue Jeans put his head on my shoulder and face against my cheek, he knew that he was too cute for words when he took the pose.

As the sun began to slide behind the rainforest side of the mountain, I made my way down to the yard with an ice pack, a torch and the beautiful hardcopy edition of *Black Beauty*. He laid down after his milk, put his head on my knee and we began. Jessie and Shanti were listening also and the story of the little black colt, an awful lot like him, became a timeless echo into the stillness of that sacred, smelly yard. He listened and he listened, then when he was almost snoring, I promised that I would come back for the next few chapters, every night.

There were these tears. Nothing was wrong. Everything was right. This was just so lovely.

I had to know more about Anna Sewell, the author of such a wonderful story and all told from the horse's perspective. The next day I did a little research. She had two broken ankles when she was quite young and spent her childhood being moved around by horses. This gave her the inspiration to write a story from the point of view of the animals she so dearly loved and relied upon. I remember reading *Black Beauty* when I was a little girl and how much it moved me. How I wanted to know more about the thoughts and feelings of horses, not just how I felt about them. Anna Sewell changed the way horses were understood by humans and how they were treated. Shortly after her book was published, the bearing rein was banned, deemed cruel and unacceptable, thanks to her work. The author died not knowing the difference her book would make not only in profitable sales, but where it counted most, improving the quality of life for horses around the world.

Blue Jeans had an ankle issue, like this author, but his leg was healing. How beautiful that this story meant the world to our story at this point in time. We were blessed to have our miracles and such a perfect summer's night. The fireflies were dancing aimlessly on the outside of the faded yard rails. Another few chapters had been shared, Blue Jeans was now snoring and the full moon was begging for just a little more. I looked deeply into the eyes of my mare and told her how grateful I was to know her son. She looked back with kindness and patience and a wisdom well beyond my years. Like most mothers, she loved it when he was sleeping. There was peace for her and thoughts of horses from faraway places. This was our country life. We were so lucky.

In the morning I woke to find the colt lying still with his body pushed through the bottom rail of the yard. I ran to his side, my heart set securely back in my throat. I thought that he was dead. He wasn't. He had tried to escape through the shade cloth again. I had deliberately hammered six more pegs to the ground in each section of the yard, to stop such an event, but somehow it came loose, and he was not looking good. I tried to move him. He would not budge. All his legs were flaccid, almost lifeless and he made a little grunt.

He was breathing very slowly. Was it a snake? Was it a tic? Was it some kind of poison? Was it colic? What on earth had happened?

I quickly filmed him with my phone and sent a message off to my vet, who could not come to the farm due to Covid restrictions and her need to isolate. I was given another vet's number to call for this emergency and was just about to make that call. I tried pouring a bucket of water over his back, to get a little response from him, when I noticed a very defined and deliberate yoga stretch coming from his front legs. A burp and then a struggle to his feet. He had gorged himself and feasted on the sweet, sweet grass through the night and like some guilty, giddy drunkard, staggered to his feet and made his way groggily back into the yard and onto his mother's milk. He scared me so much. I hugged him and hugged him. This was his fourth serious brush with the lure of death—the fourth miracle I witnessed with him on our farm. He had conquered what appeared to be a very severe colic. The kind of colic that can kill. He was given a lecture by both his mother and I ...

He had no right making silly choices like this over extra grass; especially when we had not finished reading *Black Beauty* yet; especially when we had already been through so much; especially as we loved him so much.

A few days later a wild storm broke the sky open. It did not ring ahead and ask for a visit, it just arrived. World weary trees were bent beyond reason and water poured from above like a rush of angry fire hydrants, spluttering endlessly into the earth, putting out something that just was not real or justified. The round yard began to flood.

It had been a very hot day, so at first the rain seemed like a good thing, a break from the heat. But then it wasn't good at all, it really wasn't. The little colt had nowhere to lay down, the water had risen so high so quickly. I ran down with a torch and haltered my Jess.

'Walk carefully girl, I will move you from here, go slowly, please.' She did. I had just finished building the third hospital paddock, it had a nice, easy slope, so it was not flooding.

My mare led the way and I looked over my shoulder to check that her baby was following. He was limping badly and as I secured them into the new safe space, I took a closer look. Blue Jeans' injured leg had regressed. He was almost walking on his pastern, the area of flesh above his hoof (like walking on a wrist). I checked his other front leg, it had bent even further and was struggling to hold him up and then his back legs, which had somehow now curled under more. What was going on? What had happened? I wanted to give him some bute to numb any pain, but he would not take it. He just wanted to lay down and was grateful that he could do this, with his mare standing over his tired body.

I went back to the house and I sobbed and sobbed. Something awful had crept into my heart. Something I never thought would ever be able to sneak inside, but it had. I cried out for some help. I prayed and I prayed, and I cried for help for him. Amongst all the tears and the pleas, I knew in my heart what was coming. He was suffering. He was suffering. It was real. I was going to put him down. I was not going to be able to help him any more. I was going to lose him. He was going home.

I knew all these things. I sent a text message to my vet who just happened to be coming up the next day for a check up on his healing leg, his disappearing back wound, and all the progress he had made. I let my vet know that there had been this regression and then somehow, I fell asleep, drowning and gasping in the water that was now a foot deep in that sacred round yard. There was no moon, not a firefly to be found. There was a sick, empty feeling and a little colt who was losing his battle.

I got up the next morning and went down to give him medicine. He was standing strong on all legs again. I breathed relief. I must have exaggerated the problem. I must have missed something in the dark. I hugged him and brushed him, then fed the mares. But after a couple of hours, things were dire once more. I blocked them out. I was waiting for the vet. We would get an operation. I had my superannuation. I would get onto that company again and tell them once more that this was a rural emergency. This horse needed the best of care. My mind made a clear plan, as I waited for the vet to arrive.

I did not want to look down. I looked up at his beautiful face. I kissed his eyelids and told him how special he was. I brushed his little white wings and the fluffy racoon tail. I brushed his whole body, even the legs, that were all seriously compromised now. I brushed them gently and pushed any hard thoughts away. I had to look after him. He was counting on me to look after him.

I could hear the vet's vehicle making its way up the dirt road towards our farm gate. Suddenly, Blue Jeans put his head up on my shoulder. He had to reach slightly uphill in this new sloping hospital paddock. He was like a giraffe at the zoo, reaching for leaves from a high tree. He stretched his neck, and he folded his muzzle in behind my upper back. He hugged me for a very long time. I looked over at him and he had his eyes closed tightly. I checked my heart, and it was like a petrol bowser, overflowing at the tank, with his superb brand of love. He poured out everything he had in that little foal chest. I thanked him and without a second thought, he moved from me down to his Aunty Shanti, who was in the aligning paddock, and did exactly the same thing. He hugged her tight.

As the vet approached the paddock, we talked about his progress and the message I had sent last night. I relayed that I had this feeling about him that would not shift. She took a look at his legs and they were all failing. I began crying. I could not talk properly any more. Words came out like spurts of pain, spears of defeat, choking sadness. I said something about, having to make a choice because of a Higher Love we feel for someone special.

My vet stood strong and centred, calm and compassionate. I asked her to be completely honest with me about his chances for survival, an operation, anything. Could he be helped from here? She said nothing. She moved her head slowly and gently, from side to side, signally 'no'. I will never be more grateful for this silent conversation and the thoughtful way that she delivered it. I had somehow already made the decision inside and she assured me that it was correct. He would be put down. Now. No more suffering for this fella.

The vet explained the equinology before us. Blue Jeans had been healing but his body was now thriving at almost three months old. The weight of his proud and magnificent developing form had put weight on his fragile leg and all other legs that were working overtime to keep him standing. He could not grow slowly, and his legs could not speed up their healing. Nature had overruled any dreamy, hopeful thoughts a young horse girl might have held. Life, and its beauty and wonder, was taking life. The clarity of the situation at hand, crept up into my mind and out through my heavy heart like a strike from a menacing viper. I was deep inside the poison of a dark and lurid dream. One I could not wake up from.

I rang a dear neighbour and asked for help with his tractor—I asked if he would bury my colt. My colt was still alive when I spoke this sentence that did not feel good at all. It did not seem to be in order with the running of the universe. It wasn't. My neighbour Jed responded immediately. He would be on my farm within an hour and a half.

My vet explained to me clearly what would need to be in place and how Blue Jeans would be put down. I listened intently and I moved through the motions, completely focused on one goal and one goal only, not to stop the process. To see every single minute through.

First, I had to halter my mare and halter him. He came straight to me. He let me slip that little blue halter over him with the trust of a little lamb. As I fastened the buckle I screamed so deeply inside somewhere. Nobody could hear, only God. I had spent weeks building up this trust with him. *You can trust me boy with a halter. You can.* But I realised that I had been training him for his death. Without the halter, the rest could not happen easily. He came to me and I knew that fastening the halter sealed his fate. The same hands that had helped bring him into the world during that hard labour, were now the hands that were going to kill him. I struggled with that instantly, but I stayed on course, because I loved him. He looked at me with all the innocence of a child. There were tears running down my cheeks, but he was happy to be a good horse and put on his halter. He was like *Black Beauty*. He trusted this human.

My mare was given a needle to sedate her. She stood right near her baby, the vet and me. She was already calm, perhaps she knew something ahead of time. I don't know. Blue Jeans was given a needle to sedate him. He stood quietly, then the vet brought out a very big syringe, about a foot long, and almost two inches wide. It was filled with a bright green fluid. It was the ugly needle; the medicine that killed. I asked. I wanted to know how. It was potassium and it would stop his heart.

As the green disappeared from the syringe, slowly oozing into the neck of my baby horse, I watched it inch for inch, mesmerized and caught up in a space I have never been. I felt like I was the fluid, I was doing this to him. It was an invasion that could not be altered. It was surreal and consumed me like a horror movie. I had turned to stone. I could not turn it off.

Blue Jeans fell backwards first. His hind legs bent on the warm grass. Then his front legs. He went to his side now and it had been gentle that moment when he fell. It was like slow motion. I looked into his eyes and held onto his chest and injured leg. He was with me, then he left. His eyes glazed over and his body went still.

The vet checked for a heartbeat and he was gone, 'galloping in the sky', she said. I really hoped so. My heart just broke again and again, like it would never ever stop. I did not feel his spirit or feel anything biblical or spiritual. I felt nothing but the deepest sadness. I thanked the vet, we shared a hug and I waved goodbye as she left the horrid crime scene. It was a kind death, but it was still a death and something about making this decision on a baby that was breathing a little while ago, did not sit well inside me, despite knowing that it was correct.

I sat with my little man and watched the beautiful white section of his mane, floating above his painted wings in the breeze. The movement made him appear to be only sleeping. I looked at his strong, round, Quarter Horse rump, so powerful and pronounced even in death. He was majestic. There were little birds flying around the wire on the fence just near him. I thought about this paddock. I was so determined to get the third one done, it seemed so important at the time. This was the paddock that would help prepare him for mountain life. No. It was the paddock that he would die in.

Blue Jeans had just died. I was gone. I was me, breathing and crying, but I felt dead. I knew that in a little while, I had to move his mother. She did not paw at him or investigate his stillness. She eagerly left the paddock under halter and joined Shanti for a wild gallop across the mountain in our open field. Jess came back once or twice to check that I was still sitting with her colt. She trusted me. I would stay with him. He was safe.

I heard the tractor making its way up the hill, it seemed like an eternity had passed. I was glued to the ground. I looked over at my little mate's body. Still beautiful. Still wings. I knew that he had to be buried swiftly. I was so grateful for the help I received that day. Jed took the greatest care with him, as I walked back to the house and tried to scramble through my messed-up thoughts. It had been a very hard day.

Later that evening I went and sat by the new grave. I felt numb. I just could not really picture him in the ground. I walked down to talk with Jess, who was now calling frantically for her baby, even though she had watched him being buried. I talked to her about what had happened and told her why I had sent him home, back to the *Pastures of Light*. I told her the story twice, because just like me, her heart was numb. It just did not make any sense. He had been such a fighter, he had overcome every single obstacle, he was so beautiful. Why wasn't he here? Why him? She trusted me with this story and went back to grazing and accepting the saddest day we have ever known together. The day her baby died.

A miracle birth and magical discovery there are two white wings painted on the foal's shoulders.

Mother and Son.

Blue Jeans is 10 hours old. His black coat has turned sorrel.

Xmas in a stable. *Blue Jeans* at 6 weeks old.

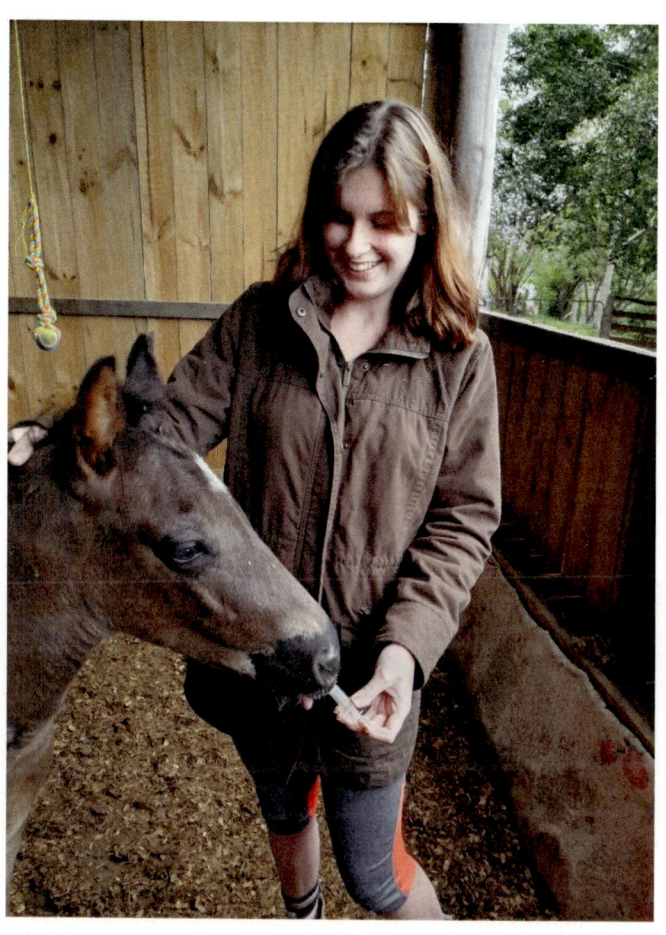

Our colt will only willingly take medicine from my daughter, Leilani, a teacher of little children.

Angel in a round yard. First evening out of the stable. He made it slowly and safely down the hill with a very fragile leg.

Two and a half months old, brown baby coat is falling off, jet black coat pushing through, leg is healing.

First day in his hospital paddock. Rug made for him by grandma while he was in his dam's womb.

Blue Jeans and his dam, *Jessie*, two and a half months old and losing his baby coat.

A love that never ends.

Blue Jeans and *Bron* in the last days of Summer and four days before he passed.

Deceased colt is tucked into Shanti's shoulder on the right, surrounded by a circle of golden light. You need to zoom in (might need to enlarge this image.

Blue circle shows the location

Blue Jeans' face is super-imposed on the tiny grey feather alongside the blue central feather. (Hope Feathers collected during his time with us).

Black foal image sitting in the centre of our Mango tree, photo taken by grandma two weeks before he was born.

(note it is easier to see the image if the picture is kept at this size)

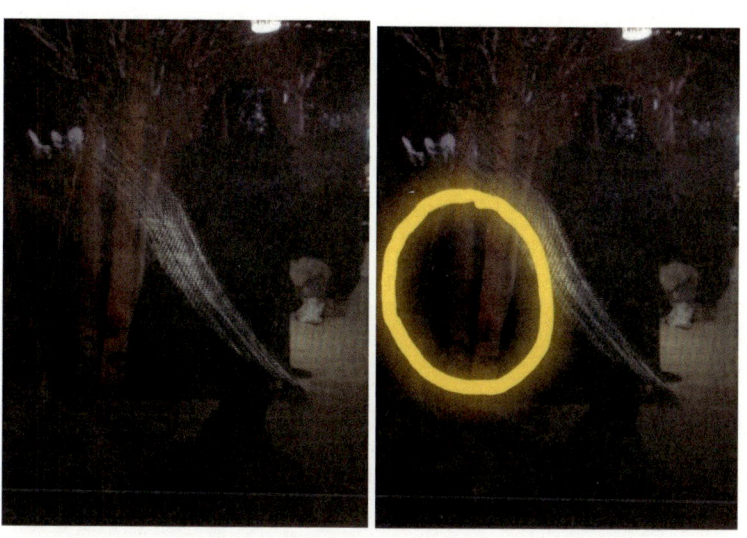

White wing painted on bedroom screen window Mother's Day (cannot be explained). *Blue Jeans* face super-imposed under the wing and onto an outside tree trunk – May need to zoom in.

Blue Jeans as he appears in Horse Heaven. A blue colour permeates through his jet-black coat.

Angels sing personalized harmonies to horses that lift their pain and suffering.

A single sunflower blooms surprisingly at the stables shortly after his death.

Blue Jeans lives in a field in Horse Heaven surrounded by these beautiful flowers.

Heavenly pastures on Earth, our farm, *Tahoma.*

There is no garden at our stables.

Aunty Shanti loves having her mane braided as we await the arrival of a lifelong dream

Jessie at her most beautiful and three weeks over her due date. A foal is born by the end of this day

Bron visiting her uncle's farm and *in love* at nine years old with *Starlight*.

Bron at fifteen on her beloved Quarter Horse, *Beau*.

Chapter 10
The Golden Room

Shanti folded her neck around Jess and shadowed her every move, granting us the greatest of compassion and support. Shanti was very aware of the suffering on the mountain that day and was also grieving the loss of her little nephew. She loved him too. He had hugged her for so long and hugged me for so long. I realized something very clearly in that moment of recall. He had known that this was his last day. He had known that he was going. He was saying goodbye. He made sure that he let us all know. It meant the world, but it still hurt so much.

I am lucky to live in the country, even though you can be asked to endure very hard days like this one. I had my dearest country friend on my doorstep the next day with dinner, flowers and arms that held up my tired, sobbing body. I just cried and cried, and it was a cruel, merciless river churning and ripping through my sides. It was full of absolute despair, full of every single loving moment with an Angel. Somebody so dear was missing.

My childhood friend was coming up from Newcastle to stay for a couple of days. She was going to meet him for the very first time but now she wasn't.

She brought dinner, lollies and a history of friendship that did not require any light conversation. She caught all my mixed-up words, my struggle for reason, my shock, my sorrow. Dayna took some photos of the farm and one of those photos was of my two mares. As she shared the image, it suddenly caught my attention.

In this photograph of Shanti and Jess there was an orb to one side of Shanti's shoulder. I made a comment about how spirits do that sometimes, maybe his spirit was around and then I quickly forgot about it. My dear friend left but sent me a digital copy of that picture. I had been crying for days now it seemed. I had a week to go before I would be back in a busy classroom teaching. I was a mess. I was in an ever-sliding quicksand of grief.

I just could not feel him. I have a faith, but I could not feel him in my soul or even in my memory. All I felt was the emptiness and the loss. Hollow, vacant, dead. My mare was very good, she was settled and at peace again. I wasn't. I was caught somewhere inside the green syringe and the little blue halter.

Then one night, the tears stopped. Just for a little while, I drew a breath. I fell asleep that evening and felt my spiritual body being lifted from my physical body. I was travelling swiftly in this golden, swirling light, with tiny golden flecks inside it, like a million brilliantly shiny gold leaf remnants. I knew that I was astral travelling and was not startled by this at all, because it had been a natural part of my life since I was very little. I knew that I had left my body, my bedroom, the farm and I was now in Heaven, standing in a room surrounded by this gold. In the room I saw three people. They were there waiting for me to arrive. My late father, my miscarried son, and my little Blue Jeans. They were all there together. No words were spoken between us, but I picked up my son, who was wrapped in a cotton swathe as a newborn baby boy. I had time to hold him. I remembered it all.

I came back to my sleeping body and realized what had just happened. I was so grateful that my dad knew my son, and my son knew my colt, and they all knew each other and were together in the other world. I felt grateful that God had let me go home just for a moment to see them all and to see my little horse which somehow still seemed to be breaking my heart. It did not stop the tears at all, it just brought a huge level of understanding and peace somewhere. If this was how it was going to be, then this was how it was going to be. I had lost all these people to death in different ways, at different times and I had grieved them.

I thought about the baby I lost at the end of my first trimester, when my daughter was two-years-old. I had called him Kai. I had wanted him so much, but he died inside me. I never got to hold him or raise him. I cried a very long time for my unborn son.

I thought about my father who had died slowly in hospital after his fourth stroke. The way our family sat around his wailing bed and laughed and cried and included him in our farewell conversations. When he left, the lights went out. I would saddle my Jess and head over the mountains with flowers for a father that I knew I could never stop missing. Here he was now with my son and my colt.

I thought about the photo that my good friend took and the swirling light in the orb. I went back and took a closer look, zooming in on that section of the image. I found the same golden flecks I had seen in the room in Heaven, and then I gasped. Deep into the side, just off the shoulder of my daughter's horse, Shanti, was a tiny foal face embedded amongst the swirling light. It was Blue Jeans. His spirit had somehow, quite miraculously, turned up in a photo taken three days after he had died. It was him.

I lifted inside. He had been around us. He'd been around his Dam and his Aunty and he had been waiting for me patiently, to visit him in Heaven. My mind was spinning wildly and my heart began filling with joy. Oh, this is love. This is what love can do. When all seems lost, it is really, really, just another step away. Really. Another miracle to bear. Oh, how can we bear them? So many. We must acknowledge them. They are there, even when all feels lost to us and gone, they are there.

That afternoon, I saw him again briefly. I was awake, but I was given another vision, a chance to go near those *Pastures of Light* once more. He wasn't with the other horses or the Angels, he was grazing alone in a pale, wheat-colored field. The wind picked up his beautiful features and played with them, his magical wings, his racoon tail, his fluffy mane, while I glanced at my dearest of dearest.

He was taller, sturdier and I noticed instantly that all legs were straight, strong, and healed. He grazed, then he raised his thick neck, glancing at me briefly before turning across his body and gazing off into the distance, exactly like what a horse would do in the wild. He was free and happy and contained.

He did not need me. I was the needy one. I really was. I needed him all the time.

I was given so much. I will never lose the details of the vision and it is as clear today, as the moment I first saw it. It was an image perhaps already set on my heart, a long, long time ago. The features of the most beautiful horse. The horse I had dreamed about when I was ten-years-old. It was the one I had hoped to find; the one that was born with wings; the one that I had loved.

It was proof of a timeless innocence and bond that existed between a girl and a foal. The vision was over almost as quickly as it had appeared. I looked at him until he faded back into that other world, and I faded back into mine … and an Angel whispered to me that Blue Jeans was just passing time.

Chapter 11
What Lies Beneath the Skin

Our days were long and summer was at its peak. The air was as hot as a trillion burning coals yet laced with liquid that constantly drew the water from your damp body. Humidity equals dehydration. I had not had a drink from our waterhole since my boy was born. Bron kept up our water day and night in two round tubs, but I longed to swim underwater, across the dam like I did each summer. I missed the feeling of being completely weightless and submerged in the cool. I was a water baby trapped in a blistering desert.

I stood patiently under the hose as my Keeper washed us down and I was thankful for the trees that grew in the paddock behind our yard. We would walk over slowly and spend the afternoons during heatwave days, catching a tiny cool breeze that crept up from the nearby river. My baby knew what to do. Bron had his leg strapped up with an ice-cold poultice from her fridge and he would find the darkest corners of the mango tree canopy, flick his tail at butterflies and dream his little boy dreams.

She was watching us. She never left our side. I glanced to see my Keeper with peace across her face and joy riding in her heart as we went about our afternoon, escaping the intensity of the sun. Why was she so earnest at times? Everything Bron felt, I also felt. We had a bond so deep, and I knew she loved Blue Jeans, almost as if he was her own born son. He loved her in the same sure way. He looked for her each day and when she was not in the yard, he talked about her constantly. What she did, what she said.

Horses can read thoughts. We often speak through telepathic communication, and we listen with the greatest sensitivity. We could hear her thoughts. Her mind was always racing lately. She wanted to keep us all safe and she wanted to help my boy. I had watched Bron deliver him when my labour became complicated. She had also taken close care of his leg as the fractured bones were mending, during our long time in the stables. When his back tore open, it was our Keeper that tended to the horror and pain of that mess. Then when he slipped under the yard rail one night, determined to get to more grass, she got him out of his drunken stupor and onto his legs just in time. Having her around always made me feel that we had a set of human hands willing to reach in for us and a heart that knew no boundaries. I wanted my son to grow up knowing this about people. Of course, it is not always the story that horses will have, but we are big and human beings are small, we must take care with them. Blue Jeans understood.

I knew my son was special, most mothers feel this way. I knew there was more to him than what could be seen on the outside. His spirit was old and his voice was different to any horse I had ever talked to before. He told me things about the other world I had not yet learned. The world where we all came from. Blue Jeans remembered all his friends in Heaven and he remembered meeting me when I was Beau. He knew Shanti also and he knew horses that we had both met along our way here with different people. He seemed to know how the networking here and there operated. Horses would share their stories of humans, much like humans shared their stories of horses. We got to learn about human care as horses, because we pooled our information, grew in knowledge and were willing to listen to different points of view.

Every now and then we would rub shoulders with an absolute expert in the paddock who usually turned out to know absolutely, not much at all. Listening, observing, and sharing was key. Human beings were odd at times. They wanted to understand us, but they often went about it in the wrong way. My Keeper had tripped like this many times. She was all heart. She could not really see the bigger picture. The one that held the best payoffs for mind and soul investment. The tough moments. When she thought she was losing, she was always winning. Bron was learning.

I wanted to share everything with my Keeper, but I could only share what she was ready for. At this time, in this round yard, on these hot, hot days, I was sharing my son and he was sharing all that she was equipped inside to handle. He gave her challenge after challenge. The kind that tore at your heart. I was very aware that he was on a mission with her and every tear that spilled from The Keeper's eyes was proof that the job was being done. She was winning, so was he.

I loved the way my Bron hugged us each day and told us what we meant to her. So many horses forget to do this in their own herds. We can take each other's grazing presence for granted. I loved her bare feet and cotton dresses that swished against my legs and shoulders as she brushed my dry coat. I wanted to tell her then. I loved her so much. I looked into her soul, and I told her. *I love everything about you.*

On the night before the big storm came, my son huddled into my drowsy body. I had not exercised properly since he had been born and I felt the extra weight building around my hips and belly like a soft cushion to count on during rest. All was not lost! I was well fed, but by hand, not the paddock. I could not complain and I always ate everything put in front of me.

My little colt wanted to talk with me. I was tired but I listened. He said that he was going home, back to the spirit world and that it would happen soon. I felt my heart skip inside, I already knew that he would not be with me forever. This was shorter than I imagined but he had his reasons, there were always reasons. My son told me he had given everything he possibly could to our Keeper except for the one last thing. Blue Jeans was sure that she needed something more. He nudged against my neck and hid his eyes and ears beneath my mane. He felt the future in his heart and sadness for just a moment. He loved me.

'You will not find me, mother. You will look for me, but I will not be with you, I will go home first, then I will return to your paddock, just for a little while. It will be my spirit that is with you then, my body must go into the ground.

'She will cry a lot. She will suffer. She will need you, my dear mother. She will need Shanti. Her human heart will burst. What lies beneath her skin will run out in a torrent, like the broken side of an ocean and she will empty herself of all the hurt and sadness she has ever felt since the day that she was born. This will happen to our Keeper because my death is going to erupt everything inside her. Remember, I was her dream. She will not want to let go. But she will and it, my passing, will deeply injure the injured. It will break her.

'As horses we know that we will all see each other again. Of course, we remember *The Pastures*. I was happy for my son because I remembered them and all the love that he would be returning to'. What he realized as he was speaking to me however, changed my thinking about the order of things. Blue Jeans told me that he could not really tell the difference between Heavenly paddocks and our dirty old round yard. In his heart, the two worlds had merged. He wanted to stay with her, our Keeper. He wanted to hug her every morning and every night. He wanted to gallop over the mountains with her, manes flying with the wild, wild wind and spirits joined forever as rider and steed. He wanted to grow old with her and teach her grandchildren how to behave around horses, but he was going home. His lessons were almost complete.

They had been important challenges for her, the trials of the gauntlet, every single one. She had learned more about healing with horses. Her practical skills had grown and most essentially, her heart was now tipping over with love. Her love for horses had amplified like an ever-increasing assembly of brilliant stars on the clearest of nights. The miracles that had been witnessed by her were now richly embedded into her DNA and she had turned the harshest of circumstances into happy songs and stories by the witness of an immutable and unwearied moon. There was just one more detail to impart. It was the very experience she did not want to experience; the tyrant in her mind and heart that she was silently and ferociously fighting against. Death.

Chapter 12
This is Dying

Before I came into Bron's world, I was well rehearsed on what it was I would be facing. You could say that I was on a mission, yes, but really, I was just fulfilling a small part of a much bigger plan. There are many ways to learn about love and there are many ways to teach it. I was just one soul in one story. The story involved the soul of my dam and the soul of my Keeper. There was also an overriding soul to our story. The soul of our God or Creator. Now let me share something with you dear reader, that soul is hard to articulate. It is seen and believed in, in so many ways and forms, through so many different windows. Who am I to tell you just exactly how you will interpret that particular view? I cannot. I can say however, that we share a common ground: To feel, share, reach for and comprehend love.

Through the window of love, I slipped into your world. I came on a cause and one cause only, to teach love and to learn love. Dying had very little to do with it. It was a mere means of transportation, just like birth.

She was my beauty. She was my deepest dream. To find a girl who loved horses so much, she would never forsake my needs. I found her. She was real but I could not keep her. I was always just passing through.

As our beautiful summer days peaked amongst the demands of a relentless sun by day and endless showers of rain by night, I knew that my time for leaving her was drawing near. My legs were giving me grief. All of them now, not just the fractured healing one. All were under strain. I did not show it to her until I absolutely had to. I wanted and I mean selfishly wanted, more of those perfect days.

She would call to me in the mornings with a sweet little voice like the cheery chirp of a pocket-sized bird. The love in her lungs would float through the air to my twitching ears and fill my body with comfort and joy. As soon as she opened the heavy yard gate, I would walk to her and hug her, trying my best to return all that she had given to me. We had an understanding. It was silent and yet it was bellowing loudly from every corner of the mountainside. Our love was as strong as the wilderness. It thrived on all that was natural and raw and real. It could never be broken—of that I knew deep in my core. All that was Heavenly glued it together, no matter what challenges had been faced. It was unshakeable; a song between us, a duet everlasting.

I spoke with my mother and prepared myself for the storm that was always coming. But there was a whole lot more going on behind the scenes. The night before I was to leave, the Angels from *The Pastures* came to visit me. They filled our round yard in a flux, like an annual country meeting. All had long wings that swooped and draped across the crusty earth. Male and female, tall and short, they glowed iridescently against the blackened sky with just a hint of moonlight shining onto their shoulders. This also lit their faces and my Aunty and my mother were mesmerized by the beauty that shone from every cheekbone and curve of their eternal smiles. All was abuzz on the mountain farm, while our Keeper slept peacefully, quite unaware of the events that were about to unfold.

They wanted to talk about her in great detail, because they knew that my leaving would turn her heart. They whispered gentle words of praise for all that had been happening in the almost three months since I was born. They had been watching from the big screen back home and were thrilled to be standing in the one place that had been the source of such wonder and inspiration. As Angels do, they began to sing and harmonize the Rainbow tune she had fumbled with on those nights when my legs needed comfort and my eyes drifted off into hazy dreams. The Angels were happy with how everything had worked out. They stroked my dam and told her how proud they were of her, telling my mother not to worry, I would come back to her in spirit, but my body was needing rest now. I had lived it out as best I could.

I wanted to hear news of my friends in Heaven and before I could even ask the words, I heard their voices calling to me and saying how much they had enjoyed my Earth story. Every detail was known in Heaven. Every gentle moment and every harsh reality. They were part of it and deeply invested in the days to come.

All human/animal connections are just like this. People often think that they go to a pet store to find their new friend, or they stumble across a stray and bring someone home, but it works in the reverse. The animals choose the humans. We choose them and then we make plans from Heaven on how to enter their lives. The Angels help us with these plans but manoeuvring prospective animal owners into the right place and the right time can be tricky business. Love appears before the human in the shape of their most desired companion and love cannot be rejected. Many times humans didn't even know they were going to be hoodwinked, rounded up, entangled, but once they saw us, it was always game over. At some point, all animals must return to their Heavenly homes. For horses, it is *The Pastures*, for dogs and cats, it is something similar and akin to their natural and preferred environment, also upheld and cared for by Angels.

I knew that Bron had other loves from her life in the world where I came from. Because they were attached to her through their hearts, they could be part of the story she was living now. So could the humans who had left her side. Her father was in the human part of Heaven, but he knew me. He knew that I was always coming to be her foal. He had been there at my birth when she checked on my name. Her father was aware that things were about to get very hard for his little girl, that little horse girl he had taken to riding schools and watched gallop up the hall to bed each night. He knew she was about to suffer.

But Angels bring us glue and hope and praise. They sing our songs so that we might remember not to feel so sad when things must end. I had my wings painted on me for a reason. I had to tell her somehow, not to be so sad. She was going to feel the deepest of sad, sad songs. I was going to listen to that song very soon and all around me began to feel like my past, while I prepared her to let me go. The Angels stayed until the hint of morning crept over the highest ridge. I was ready.

She had no idea that things were about to change so drastically. I had to hold myself together, not to give an ounce of evidence that my pain had increased. I pushed down hard on my legs so that there was no obvious limp, but to the trained eye, you would see that the muscles in my chest and rump were contracted. I was holding it in until I could hold no more. The day had been very hot once more and she had taken us over to the shade of the mango tree. By the time we were back in our round yard, the storm had begun.

She turned and saw the fold in my front leg. I had lifted it up onto the toe of my hoof, but I could not hold the rest of my body up any longer. She gasped. So, I straightened my leg out again and she pushed it away, out of her mind. At first, she denied seeing it. I was glad.

As the ground of the yard began to fill with water and the night turned black once more, she came back down into the yard with a torch and haltered my mother. I could not lay down in the deep pool that was now forming around me and she had realised that I needed to get off my legs. Her third hospital paddock had just been completed. It was only a few steps across the driveway. We could make it and there was no flooding on the ground because of the slight slope. As we walked with her to drier ground, she turned and saw my crippling legs, all folding beneath me. It tore at her heart as it tore at me. It was known in that moment in the same way a spear would pierce a soldier in battle. Death was known. We both pushed it away and out of our minds. I looked into her beautiful eyes and somehow it blocked out the throbbing agony. She wanted to give me medicine for pain, but all I wanted was to lie on the earth with my mother close by. The rain poured down relentlessly pounding at the seams of our story. I heard her crying through the night. I heard her desperate pleas to our Greater God for mercy for my life. For another miracle. She was already grieving my passing and I was grieving losing one single day that belonged to our future here. I was very aware that I would not be staying. Everything was working to plan.

I did not pray and ask to stay. I made a Higher choice, the choice that comes when you love something or somebody so much. You do not ask for yourself, you ask for them. What is best for them. The best thing that

I could ever give to my Bron, was to teach her about love and then to take that love back to Heaven. To die. Now I cannot tell you exactly why that is, but I can tell you, it was the plan and because of love, I was sticking to the plan.

She woke up and checked me the next morning, convincing herself that she must have things wrong. I was such a fighter and I had overcome every single slight in my life up until now. She was going to organise an operation for my leg or legs, whatever was needed, she was going after it. But by the middle of the day, her heart was sinking into those messy depths once more, as my legs very seriously began to fail me.

She brushed my body from head to crippled hoof, kissed my eyelids, told me I was the most beautiful horse she had ever known, whispered my name deep into my soul. The time was near for our goodbye. She still did not know for sure, but she did. She was shaking from head to hoof. She was a part of me and I was a part of her. I took those tremors from her body and filled them with all the love I had left in my heart. I stumbled up the slope to her and hugged her tightly, for a longer time than usual. My spirit was heavy with sadness to leave her, but I could not let on that I was suffering in this way. I had to be strong. Stronger than her. I pretended it was just another day and therefore, she could not feel anything but joy from me. It put a buffer on the horrible sting that was building between us.

I knew that my death would be quick, so when the first needle went in, the sedative to stop me from running, I just stayed close to her. I made sure she could feel the warmth of my body on her skin. That same warmth she had felt at my birth, was now with her at the doorstep of death. I was with her. Then I felt myself drop to the ground, she reached out and put her hands on my chest, my heart, my shoulder and my leg. She stayed with me, sat down with me, as my eyes glazed over, my muzzle dropped open and my spirit flew high to the world that was calling me home. I was death in her open palms, I was death in her sinking mind, and I was death in the rupture of her beautiful heart. I was gone.

Can I tell you, it was the most loving experience of my life to die with Bron holding me this way—I never felt more alive, loved or cared for. It was, in a way, like my birth. She was there in the very beginning, and she was there right to the very end. I was exceptionally and lovingly bookended by the human horse girl.

She stayed with my body for a long time, until her friend came to bury me. I could see her from Heaven, breaking her heart over losing me. But I was alive, of course I was. I had just moved a paddock away.

I wanted to call to her, but she could not hear anything. She was numb to the core and in a sense, my Keeper was also dying. She was drowning in another kind of storm. This was not the story she believed in. Her dreams were different than the one before her eyes right now. She had dreamed of a life with a beautiful colt. I was no longer in her world.

I tried for days to reach her, but she had shut down inside. The Angels sang the Rainbow song and the song she wrote about me and played on her guitar. They hummed this to her through the mornings and she could hear them, but she shut it out. It hurt so much. Feathers continued to fall at her feet ... she wanted me, not feathers. From Heaven we can send signs. I was given permission to turn up in a photo and it helped a little. I had been spending time with my dam and my Aunty in my spirit body just as I had promised I would. They were so pleased to see me, and my mother went back to happy grazing days, no more searching for her baby. My Bron was not there yet. She had a faith and a spiritual understanding, but she was shattered inside and these ruinous heartbreaks take time to mend.

Just as she had always been there for me, I was now with her. She could not see me or hear me. I wanted her to. I shuffled up beside her as she cleared out the round yard, packed up the feed bins, folded the shade sail, shovelled old piles of manure. I was right there beside her just as I had always been, but she did not feel a thing.

This is dying. This is what happens, and it is as natural and as important as the day we are born. We live, we breathe and then we finish. My time was for three months as a black colt with white wings. A baby horse that she would absolutely adore was going to be taken from her in one of the cruellest ways. This is dying.

Loving someone so much that you just cannot bear life without them. Crying so hard that your sides quake and you wonder if the tears can ever be halted. They never can.

She was dying unto Him. Her core was breaking and making its way back to the Keeper of all Keepers. Her spiritual death came about because she was losing someone, she loved more than she could ever explain. Her God, her Creator, her Carer had also somehow spent moments with her around the timing of a beautiful dream horse. All the love of Heaven had entered the world with Blue Jeans. The only way back to joy and peace after shock and grief was to acknowledge where he had really come from.

Where I dwell, my dear reader, is not in some wayward side of the universe or above the clouds in a stern judgement seat, but in the hearts and souls of every created being. I am awakened from my blissful sleep by the call of a pure love that rattles and chimes amongst my dreams. I am slumbering with you and within you. These were the words that echoed through my horse's heart. I was the looking glass of her soul. We were one of the same.

Now I had left the picture and all the heartbreak and grief—the proof of the love within her, well it made our story possible, and it will recreate the narrative again and again and again.

For this is dying. This is death. Being willing to trudge through the corridors of pain, no matter what. To do this without hesitation, is to aim very high in hopes of something. Love comes at a great, great cost. It also comes full of unfathomable miracles. It arrives and it leaves at the very best time. She was ready to meet me, so I was born into her life. She was ready to lose me, so I left. I never did either one of these things to cause her pain.

All the pain she has felt in her heart is part of an illusion that we live separately. We do not. I am as much alive in Bron now, as the days that I was with her on her mountain farm. I am buried just down from the round yard where she has planted a tree for me. A flamboyant poinciana tree that promises to produce bright red flowers each spring—the new tree on the farm that she plans to sit under from time to time and talk with me. I am vibrantly alive in her soul. There could be no greater experience than to live the full circle of life, death and then life after all of that. It is rich and real and rotten to its every core.

I will be with her in the physical way again. We have much more to share. But for now, I am kept so deeply beneath the carefully folded crevices of her healing heart. She touches me there, brushes my coat, kisses my eyelids, pats my wings. She loves me so dearly. How could I ever not feel special? I am very, very blessed.

My name is Elijah Blue Jeans.

On one sweet country night I saw an opportunity—a prospect, for change. I broke from my eternal dreaming, tidied up my celestial affairs and put on a different outfit. Without pause or concern for deadlines, I waved to My beloved as I left the Mighty office. I made a very determined journey through my glorious collection of stars and into the body of a good friend of mine who had decided to venture onto Earth as a little black colt. You could say that we shared residence. I was everywhere you can imagine; inside, outside, above, beneath, amongst the dirt in the round yard and the soft feathers that fell before her feet. I was wide awake now from the blissful fog of Heavenly imagining. Luminous, alive, the unmistakeable extra light humbly positioned within the body of a young horse.

'Why?' you might ask.

Well, I did this because of the way My love works.

I did this because I can.

PART 4

Chapter 13
Reverie

Three months had passed since my colt's death. I sat on the side of the mountain and watched our two mares grazing rhythmically and peacefully in the lush, rain-soaked, paddock.

I hugged them and combed their manes and tails. Life was as it was. The chill autumn air rushed up from the valley below and cooled my skin. Molly sat next to me panting at the picture before us. Such beauty on this farm, so many everchanging snapshots of nature now on dusk. Everything was going still, including the heartbeat of the saddest days past.

He would have been six months old at this time and ready to be weaned off his mother. I wondered for a moment what Blue Jeans would look like right now in the paddock around me. What a handsome young horse he would be: Longer legs, jet black coat, bigger white wings, black and white mane flickering in the breeze, and I glanced a maturity in his eyes, just for a second, as if he were here with us all and reading my thoughts.

My abrupt return to work shortly after his death had been like living inside perpetual numbness. I was split apart from my body somehow, just barely there and I had to relay brief details of his death to students and colleagues, the same beautiful souls who had been so invested and excited about his arrival and subsequent healing. I could not speak these words without going swiftly back inside the suffering and the horror. I will never forget the compassion that met my sorrow. Teachers who cried with me, students who made their way to my classroom to tell me personally how sorry they were that Blue Jeans had died.

So many times, I have tried to make sense of his story. I get close to understanding something and then I fall back into a fog of confusion, scrambling through this murky, unanswered deluge. Who was he? Why did he leave? Why all the suffering? Why can't he be here?

A good friend told me not to ask the *why* question. Instead ask *what did I learn*? As much as I understand that spiritual viewpoint and how much healthier that perspective is, I just do not like it, really. I would like an answer to *why*. I guess that is only human. I have noticed that my mare, his mother, does not need the answer. She accepts that he is not grazing with her and in her wisdom and grace, continues to live a full and happy life chomping away at the grass about her.

There has been so much rain of late and serious flooding in parts of the state that I live in. Thousands of people have lost their homes and all their belongings. We have just endured two years of a Covid pandemic that has also claimed millions of lives around the world.

I thought about climate change and the suffering around me. Is the Earth crying? Are we all crying? Are we slowly submerging through these tears of rain, trapped within a sorrowful vault of existence right now? What stories do others hold in their hearts?

My heart carries a heaviness in it that threatens to pour out, like a gorged dam, without the slightest of courtesies or warnings. So many times, I have sobbed privately and publicly over the loss of my dearest little man. My body shakes, my heart snaps open and there is another kind of flood taking place, causing all kinds of devastation to the landscape of my soul. I wonder when it will end.

I cannot explain to others or even myself, why I hold these feelings about him. What he meant to me, does not have a textbook definition, a biblical metaphor, or a sophisticated psychological angle. No matter what people may share or offer, it still does not resonate with the deeper truth. It is hidden from me at this time.

I look at the whole picture and I can see quite clearly and rationally that through this foal I experienced the full cycle of existence: Life, death and life after death. Logically this makes some kind of sense. But when I remember him, the emotion takes over and I look everywhere for a glimpse that the dream we shared, the dream of his life in my life, that held sadness and shock within it, was not completely real. That somehow there was a twist. He did not die. It never happened.

There have been moments when I have even expected his little body to push the dirt up from where he is buried and spring on healed legs before me, as if it were all some kind of hoax. I let my mind go there for a few minutes. I look down at the broken earth, then up at a miracle before me, with tiny white wings and eyes that tell me he is back. There is something in my spirit that assures me this is not some wayward daydream. This could happen. I am not sold on the idea that the story of him has ended. I believe that he is meant to be here and whether that's wishful thinking, or denial, or one very big step out of reality … it is the only truth where I find peace.

I glance out my bedroom window and expect to see him standing in front of the rose garden I made when my father died. I expect to find Blue Jeans there, little face inquisitively looking back through the window at me.

And so, when we cannot have our answers, something else must come our way. There were so many feathers on the ground around the time that he was with us, that asked me to pick them up and remember something. They always spoke to me of hope. I kept them. I carefully planted each one into the dirt within a tiny pink teacup that sits on my kitchen windowsill. All the hope I managed to find, assembled now before my eyes. *Hope* looks like a craft project.

I had a dream some nights ago that I was very old. My body was much smaller, and I had long grey plaits in my hair. I was walking down a road wearing crumpled trousers, an old t-shirt and comfortable sandshoes with these delicate little shoulders that were slightly hunched. I thought that I must have been in my eighties. A big red horse walked up to me and bent down on one leg so that I could climb up onto his back. I was riding him without a bridle or a saddle and as we went down the road together, all these other horses came up to greet us. Some were in tiny paddocks, some were roaming free; some small ponies, some large draft horses—there were all different breeds and colors.

We stopped under a canopy of plush, crackling trees. More horses came up to us. They talked internally, telepathically to him and then he, the big red horse, spoke this way to me. He told me what they needed. One horse needed medicine, another needed a poultice, another needed extra kind words and a warm rug, another needed to be stroked and assured. I took note of the needs before me as we made our way down the road together.

I reached down and wrapped my frail arms around the neck of this horse I was riding, burying my face into his lustrous mane. As I hugged him, he hugged me back with his gigantic heart and I knew that it was him. It was Blue Jeans. I looked up at the trees again, they were the same trees that I have only just planted in his little hospital paddocks over the months since his passing. They were now all fully grown and bending brilliantly across the driveway of home. He walked me back up to my cottage on the top of the mountain and bowed down to the ground so that I could gently slide off, landing comfortably on my feet in my neat little sandshoes. We were together again. Separation was now a very old song. Everything felt warm and natural once more.

Chapter 14
The Pastures

The school term had ended, and I left work drained and exhausted. I had been holding it together emotionally as best I could, but now I was able to relax. The minute that I turned into the drive, my eyes were searching for him. He was supposed to be with us. The heavy gate on the round yard swung stoically against a picture of emptiness.

I struggled through the night with fever and aching bones only to confirm that I had acquired Covid-19 as a parting gift from a busy term of teaching. The next few days brought about a new kind of battle. This thing, this pandemic, was bloody horrible. All of me felt seriously smashed and pelted.

I was alone. I was so, so sick and I was all alone.

I drifted between places in my mind. I seemed to be reflecting on little moments in my life. Was I going to die? Who would know? The remoteness of my country home now really isolated me in every sense, from everyone and everything.

The days that followed were languid and surreal. Suffocating. I walked outside for a while, to draw some fresh air from the mountain and then collapsed back on my bed, unable to move my arms and legs. Everything hurt.

On the fourth day, I made it to my deck, sitting propped up by pillows that prevented my lungs from accumulating more broken glass. That is how it felt in my chest, as if I were breathing in tiny splinters.

I glanced out across the land and suddenly I was staring downward, directly at dry ground moving rapidly beneath me. I was galloping or rather, a horse was galloping and I was inside them, galloping with them. It was him again. Had he known that I would be sick? It was a welcome distraction. I looked up and out and once more, I felt myself being drawn inside the spirit of my colt. He was taller, stronger and his legs were swift and powerful. This odd occurrence only lasted briefly, then I sank back into my bed, exhausted all over again, just as so many others have been over these last couple of years. I would get through this, but it was not going to happen quickly. The pandemic took the last of what I had inside me since Blue Jeans died.

I felt this strong urge to go back into the round yard and clean things up once more. I had dumped an old gate, a hose, a shovel and a mattock in there, working to plant new trees for the small hospital paddocks. I wanted his space to be clear. Why? Well, I just do not know the answer to that. My body was very weak and my mind floating in and out of all kinds of realisms. Just being able to breathe some fresh air felt like a luxury. I wondered if I should tell someone that I had felt near to death. Then I cancelled it out. So many people had felt near to death by this thing. As far as I knew, I was alive.

I sat down in the center of the yard and took a moment. The grass had all grown back now. No evidence of flooding or cracked muddy ground. Everything seemed so vacant and still. I tried to remember him, but I could barely see him. My eyes were still burning with fever. I do not know how long I had been sitting there before a shadow cast across my shoulder and I felt my body gently crumple onto the grass around me. I had done this before on those busy country girl days when I was working hard across our land.

'Just rest,' I thought, 'Sleep here a while, you are safe, then try and walk back up to the house.'

I felt myself moving into dreaming. In this in-between space, I stepped out of my body and turned around. It was Blue Jeans in the shadow, I could see him now. He stood majestic and strong before me, snorting at the autumn air as if he owned it. He did.

I just remember crying. All the love I had ever felt for him now erupting and alive within me. I was not sick any more, I was free. I felt like him. He bowed before me in a deeply respectful gesture. He spoke to me on the inside, encouraging me to climb onto his back. Blue Jeans was not a foal any more, he was now fully grown and the minute that I leapt from the ground, I knew that

I could not possibly fall off him. Like a magnet, my spirit body was connected to the spirit of him.

He said that he wanted to take me somewhere and I looked down in awe as the beautiful white markings on either side of his shoulders, suddenly fanned open into layers of fully-fledged feathers along a wingspan well beyond my outstretched arms.

Up we went, rising into the sky and melding swiftly into the other world. The world that I knew, the mountains and valleys, the houses and city streets, simply faded. My heart was rocketing inside and as my colt cantered into this brilliant Light, I could hear and feel his story, his much bigger story, unfolding inside me. All my senses became acutely aware that Blue Jeans was just a visitor to me—and that he had this long, long history of dropping into places.

Every time I asked a question, he would provide the answer, instantaneously. I was really with him. Yes, I was. We were flying through time and space. Yes, we were. I was perfectly safe.

'I will not let you fall. Hold onto my mane, Bron, we are almost there.'

I saw so many places. Small kingdoms I guess you would say, pockets of Heaven. All built by spirit and made of spirit. Bright lights and colors and shimmering. Intricate designs and architecture I had never seen drawn before, not on Earth and not even on the map of my own imagination. There were people moving in and out of vision, whispering, humming, sighing. This was a loving place. This is where he came from.

'This is where you came from, Bron. You are home.'

And then I saw the opening to the landscape I had only briefly glimpsed so many years ago, after the Pappinbarra fires. I saw the beautiful valley of the *Pastures of Endless Light*. At first, only a few horses and a few angels, but as we drew closer, there were thousands of horses resting there and so many Angels, gliding, strolling and singing amongst them.

Blue Jeans pranced proudly and elegantly through the ethereal terrain, his rich coat interchanging from jet black to shimmering blue. Angels turned to acknowledge him and then glanced up to smile at me. I was being welcomed in and I started to hear songs that I knew in amongst their unique harmonies. The words would start, or some of the tune and then it would shift to another sound. Some of these songs were songs I had written back on the farm; some were parts of popular songs on Earth that I liked. It was unusual to say the least, but so beautiful as if it had been specifically created for this moment. I found them really comforting somewhere. Blue Jeans told me that it was medicine for me. I was quite sick. I did not feel sick.

'Spirit first, body second,' was his reply. Where was my body? Then I glanced it quickly, flopped in the center of the round yard. It was perfectly okay to leave it behind.

My dear colt brought his prancing down to a very slow amble and I was able to suddenly feel inside the hearts of every horse we passed. In an instant I knew their life story and the Angels working with them nodded back to me, *yes this is true*. I wanted to reach out to each animal, stroke them, assure them. My heart extended from my chest and I watched as a warm, pink light transferred into a horse I barely knew.

Blue Jeans was deeply satisfied by this and encouraged me to reach for more. He slowed right down again, just so that I could master telepathy and healing this way. Every now and then I was distracted by the sheer joy that I was riding him. The tips of his wings had been trailing along the ground at first, now they were fully tucked back into his white paint markings, with little feathers falling here and there behind him. I hugged him, over and over. I was so glad to be with him. He was my love. He really was my love.

I started to know things. This knowing came from every direction and was being revealed section by section. I looked back at the entrance into the Valley and saw a line-up of horses moving slowing towards *The Pastures*. The Angels were guiding them in and I noticed a couple of young people in their spirit form assisting with this beginning phase, greeting each horse with all the kindness they could muster. I understood that they were in training; they were volunteers from the human section of Heaven with a deep desire to help with a horse's transition from Earth and its own special healing needs.

The death story of each horse was known. The recent life story also, but the death story was very fresh inside the spirit of each steed. Some had had more than one death and as I peered inside, I could see images of a battlefield, a shotgun, a war and that this horse still held an old story. For some horses it was their first return and they were confused or crying. I saw a beautiful white pony with tears that kept pouring from deep brown eyes. He was sad to die and had left a little girl behind, one he really cared for. I could see the little girl's tears swimming inside his heart. I saw a horse with tears in his heart because he had been slaughtered. His death was so traumatic. He had felt fear in his veins even after he had physically died. He did not understand why his owners sent him to meet such a horror. I gasped when I thought about the plight of the innocent. How could this happen? He would need a long time in Angel care.

In this world your vision could go everywhere. I observed a tapestry of glorious fields all around, as my eyes raked the edges of the picture before me. I could see them clearly, even through mountains, tucked safely away like diorama secrets. In each field there were vibrant mixes of different colored flowers, with light blue streams coursing through soft lime grass and exquisitely designed trees. Horses were resting, grazing, socializing, living amongst their own construct of paradise. To one side there were wildflowers, to another simple daisies—roses, lavender, poppies, gerberas, daffodils, and flowers I had never seen before; brand new designs. The flowers and trees were part of the medicine. They swayed and leant into the horses, sharing all that they had to help settle and soothe world weary souls. Angels made garlands and placed them around the necks of some. I saw an old draught horse lying amongst a rainbow of hollyhocks. His thick legs curled under him, his fine beard waving in the breeze. He was smiling while he dreamed. I ventured into his resting thoughts and saw a rich life amongst the English countryside. He was remembering all the errands he once ran, pulling a bread cart to town each day. There was such pride and contentment inside his soul. His job was done.

I was able to view the anatomy of a physical horse in its spiritual blueprint. If I concentrated on the area I wanted to see, I went there. Not just visually but also, I went inside it. I could feel and understand the inner biological and metaphysical makings of the horse. The Angels consoled, stroked, whispered, and called them forward. As they walked closer, they began to remember where they had first come from and their brief moments of uncertainty or shock, turned to colossal joy.

There were so many Angels flocking around like mothers and fathers at a school recital. They loved the new horses, instantly, as if they were their own offspring. I wanted to know more about these magnificent carers. Blue Jeans turned so that I could get a closer look at the nearest one. He was reading my thoughts again. Some of the Angels had been people on Earth and some had never left *the Pastures*, ever. They were made up of this iridescent white light, yet there was this constant permeating range of colour, coursing through their structure.

'The color heals,' my colt informed. Each color has a different purpose, carries a different medicine. All the Angels were dissimilar in appearance but looked and felt so connected. They were. They were filtering information to each other constantly. The Angel that I was studying had long white braids amongst her hair and a pretty patterned headband on. This gave her a Native American Indian persona and I was told that she looked and presented this way because certain horses that were coming home today, would find it comforting and familiar. Everything was being done to bring about ease. Every fine detail. I saw Angels with smart formal jackets and some with old fashioned dresses and fancy boots. I remember seeing this bright and exuberant Angel with long white dreadlocks. They were like people, but not like people.

They had wings. These massive white wings, but they were not shown all the time. They disappeared visually, then reappeared when an Angel focused strongly on a horse. They even wrapped their wings around some horses, in particular the new arrivals that were anxious or emotional. I thought about the feathers on my kitchen windowsill. They now seemed far more significant than what I had first believed.

The Angels were regal and self-assured. They were all very confident in what they could and would do. They moved amongst horses with gentleness and grace yet carried an awesome sense of self and a mighty strength. I remember feeling safe amongst them as if they would help and protect my soul. I hardly knew them. Each horse felt like I did and looked to an Angel for reassurance, which was given instantaneously without question. Nothing to fear.

I watched as an Angel turned around to face a horse walking tentatively behind them. The Angel softened their gaze and looked deeply into the soul of the homecoming horse with all the tenderness of a timely sage.

Angels had their own small herds of about three or four horses. No more than that. Once they had gathered the arriving horses together, they would ask the horses to slowly drop to the ground, to curl their legs under their bodies. The Angels sat down with them, sometimes sitting on the back of one. They stroked their manes and they occasionally shifted their positioning, talking about the things that were important. I tuned in to one of these conversations and I heard words like:

'Your time was wonderful. I was watching and I saw how incredibly thoughtful you were. Now you have a chance to rest. You will find old friends here and there is a place to gallop when your body is not so weary. All in good time. My name is Hanalia. If you speak my name or think of me, I will be with you promptly. I am here to help you. I am so glad to see you. I have missed you.'

The dialogue was so real and loving, I knew that if I were a horse, I would be incredibly happy to be in this place. I went deeper into the understanding of the talking and the singing. This was not a quiet place and yet it felt so incredibly peaceful. Blue Jeans told me that the Angels were assimilating new arrivals into the ways of their Heavenly home by using different tones in their voice. These tones could lift out physical ailments or emotional suffering from their etheric design. They looked like horses, but they were not physical. They were like this filmy, translucent substance. I looked like this too. I was not in my body, but I looked like Bron— I guess a more sparkly version of her.

Their discourse intricately covered the importance of every experience on Earth, no matter how hard, how wonderful, or even how fleeting some moments had been. They said that strength was being developed. Strength and wisdom. When moments had passed, a horse became more sensitive than before which helped to create a deeper capacity for giving and receiving love.

In their awakening, horses knew that they were serving a much greater cause. This was not just for their friends in distant paddocks but for the humans they encountered along the way. Their service affected the whole of Creation. They were noble, that was clear, alongside the exact size and loving capacity of their drumming heart. Their nobility had created so much beauty in life. It did not matter which world they were in. Their honorable and principled demeanor made a lasting impact. All this spiritual and ethical training came from *The Pastures*, but it was also deeply embedded in their DNA.

'Yes, yes, yes!' I screamed. 'I always knew they were something else!'

I noticed a group of horses gathering to my right and sensed that they did not want to overwhelm me. They were so excited to see me. I knew none of them. They were my colt's dearest friends. They had been watching our story on Earth together and they really wanted to know me, meet me. So, I slid down off Blue Jeans' back and walked amongst a herd, just like I had done so many times on the farm amongst my own horses. Jiminy Cricket, Poncho Toto, Elleena and Frederick made a beeline for some quality time conversation. Horses let you in when they believe that you can be trusted, when they consider you one of their own. This was a herd I wanted to join and learn from. I felt so humbled and privileged. I seemed to spend hours there, listening to their stories, their wisdoms and absorbing it all, like a long-lost drink. There was always cause for celebration. They were celebrating with me about meeting me. I cannot remember very much detail from the conversations we had, they seem hazy now, but

I remember feeling so loved and so special to them all. I was impressed with the notion that all these moments shared in reunion and storytelling helped build the knowledge within every occupant, Angelic, and equine. This was what it was like to be in Horse Heaven. This was the best place in Heaven. It had to be.

I also saw the re-entry portal, the place where horses returned to Earth to be the brand-new colts or fillies born to their dams. On the far side of the Valley there was this intricate corral, constructed of Light. It was octagonal with a lace-like design dangling from each rail. The rails flickered and I saw a few horses in there with such delight inside their hearts. The Light was filling them, preparing them for that epic shift into the physical world, inside the womb of their mares. I understood that this *transition* happened at different times. A part of the horse may be forming on Earth but the whole spirit came in, just before birth. The density and the shock of the physical world was not easy on them. They needed this last bit of spiritual help from the healing Light that seemed to act like some kind of buffer or cocoon.

Angels did not usually go beyond the exit area unless it was absolutely necessary. The Angels knew the timing of a horse's physical birth and they encouraged a leap of faith, directly out of the serene pastures the departing horses had become accustomed to. They projected something with each spirit leaving. I wanted to see how this worked and Blue Jeans waited patiently for my mind to understand the process before me. He knew the questions I had, but he wanted me to come to it all myself. I was so amazed at how life began. Sparks flew as the energy increased around them. One minute the horse was standing in an etheric corral, the next they were gone, off to start the story they had been dreaming of.

The Angels were part of these dreams. They helped construct stories that matched with locations on Earth so that certain horses and humans could connect with each other and beautiful hearts could grow. Honestly, it was like a rich country field of plough and harvest. Everything had purpose. Every spirit had a story and a quest to fulfil. There was a human for each horse and a horse for each human. And then when all was complete, there were these Angels of *The Pastures* that just beamed such High intelligence and grace, straight out of some devotional dreamland.

I saw other kinds of Angels on Earth, waiting for the birth. They worked with *The Pasture Angels* and checked that each new arrival had run successfully in its planned course. In that moment, I remembered Thumbelina, the stillborn foal of our miniature mare, Mudcake. Angels had been there. They had even sent me a dream a few nights ahead, where I had gone to pat a tiny bay filly and it had disappeared off our garden path. I realized with great comfort, that I had not been alone on that horribly hard day, neither had my humble little mare or the crying that came from my paddock horses. These Angels were known as The Catchers because that is what they did, they caught new life. Birth, babies and beautiful moments, they also caught tormented souls, sinking hearts, and the deepest of sorrows. They were there with us at the very beginning, they were there at the very end. I was shown quite clearly that they were with me at Blue Jeans' problematic birth and his harrowing earthly death. I could not see them then, but I saw them now. They were the invisible salve, holding spirits upright; messengers with a mission; God's specialized swat team. I am pretty sure they were around when my father passed away.

Blue Jeans was delighted in each new discovery I made. It gave him great pleasure to hear the rhythm of my own joy rising inside me, breaking down old walls of sorrow. He whinnied and laughed at me all in one. The sound that came from him in that moment will always be with me. It resonated so deeply into my soul, as if every thought or word we have ever shared, became compacted into a simple, sweet vibration.

'I want to show you something more. You will love it. Come with me.'

I climbed back onto his back and we flew over the peak of a mountain and into a vast canyon. I heard this place before I saw what lay before my eyes: Thundering hooves, screeching, wild voices tearing at the wind. This was The Galloping Field. I looked about at the surrounding mountains and spirits from everywhere seemed to have claimed positions, coveted box seats.

They came specifically to watch the horses running. I could not take my eyes of the rumbling grounds before me. Horses of all different breeds, colors, size and temperaments. They were one huge weaving mass of flight and freedom.

Blue Jeans told me that they were healed. They were taking a victory lap. After a good gallop and a few kicks and bruises, they would be ready for some more time on Earth. I glanced into the distracted faces of the spectators and all I could see was what I imagined my own face would look like right now. Utter awe. The image of a pounded celestial landscape full of hurtling equine, truly took my breath away.

Light splintered beneath their determined hooves as they tore at the surface of the ground, ripping it apart as if it were paper. They had so much power. I looked up and I saw stars lighting the field before them. The stars knew the horses by name. The stars were connected to it all, wilfully taking part in the final healing session. I glimpsed a star, but it was too much for me to take in. I began to cry. I was not upset; it was something I could not understand at first. Then Blue Jeans explained that I was remembering the beginning of his story with me— the night that he was born. A star kept that story forever. I had looked at the reflection of my very own life story captured within the brilliant sparkle of a random star. We all had a story of safekeeping within a star. Our life was always being witnessed.

But there was more. Now I really understood my emotions being overwhelmed. It occurred to me that my little black colt had galloped in this place at some point after he had died. Blue Jeans nodded with each clear comprehension I had.

'Yes, I went for my gallop here when my four legs were all healed. It took some time in *The Pastures* and I was well cared for, then I had to use these things called legs, or rather, remember how to use them.' I realized I had never seen him gallop, but now looking at the mammoth herd before me, I got a clear idea of how Blue Jeans would have experienced the celebration of his full recovery. I felt this guilt about his time on Earth with me. He was on medicine to block the pain, but he was not free. Not like this.

Blue Jeans heard my thoughts and responded without hesitation.

'I was free. You are not seeing things clearly, Bron. I was free because I had the love that you brought me. It was 'over the top' every single day I lived on Earth, precisely ninety-two days, fourteen hours, and twenty-three minutes. It liberated me. All of me.'

With those words, I knew it was true. The power of love. We all have this power at our disposal. Why don't we use it more often? Why do we seem to forget about the freedom and the happiness it can bring to the hearts of others, to our own hearts?

I jumped off his back again and felt the Heavenly earth beneath my feet. It was as if I was standing on this lavish, living carpet, so warm and energizing. I wanted to plant myself in this place it was just amazing. Then without warning, I sensed the energy around me starting to drop. The visions I had been experiencing and the internal conversations began to ease off a little. Blue Jeans was standing to my left. He reached over and hugged me, the way he had done back on the farm. He said that there were others here, that wanted some time. All that I had learned from *The Pastures* would never leave me. I knew that to be true. I buried my face into his black and white mane and glanced at the tiny feathers on his shoulder, still proof to me, that we had just flown here, when I heard a voice filled with the greatest love, authority and kindness, call to me. I knew who this was immediately. I knew Him so well.

'Are you ready?'

That is all the voice of The Almighty said to me … Are you ready?

I was confused but assured that it would all make sense. I leapt up onto Blue Jeans' back, fearful of losing him again. He told me that I would not lose him. Had I lost him yet?

He bowed before the voice and to the whole congregation now focused on us. I did not see God, but I sure did feel Him. It was as if someone had wrapped the warmest, brightest and most loving blanket around my entire being. I was safe, I was deeply, deeply loved and there was nothing that I could ever do or experience that God would not somehow fix. These are facts I knew without question. This guy always had a master plan, and it came from the pureness of His heart, this rich and absolute place of love. I felt The Caretaker smile inside my soul when my mind traversed these somewhat enlightened thoughts. He was awfully pleased that I knew Him and that I had figured Him out, well to some degree. He thanked everyone: horses, angels, spirits for helping me. I wanted to say thank you back, but He interrupted my thoughts.

'You said thank you the day you began to look after me.'

I still wanted to say thanks. I felt so incredibly grateful and privileged. I wondered how it was that I looked after Him. I looked after Blue Jeans, so I figured He must have meant, the little bit of Light inside of everything ... that my colt was really His colt.

Then I began to weep. I knew that my time here was closing, and I was going to be carried back to the dusty old round yard. I knew that something would be so hard again in my heart. I did not want to forget one detail from Horse Heaven.

Blue Jeans said to me with such clarity, 'It will not be hard, Bron, this is a ride that you will remember.'

I considered those words for a moment and flicked through all the special rides I had had on horses through my life. There were some that stood out from others. Maybe it was the way a sleepy mist crept through the mountains as a horse expired the last of the winter air, or how a horse suddenly lunged forward to meet the full throttle of a gallop. There was this one time when I rode my daughter's horse home in the dark and these brilliant fireflies had formed a moving circle in the air before us, lighting the road ahead as we had lost track of time. How thoughtful that was. I had a storeroom, a lifetime collection of extraordinary rides, so it made sense to me, that I perhaps would never forget this one.

I glimpsed my future. From this spiritual place, I could see it so easily and I was riding my mare Jess again. It would not happen straight away. We had been missing him for a long time. She was so worked up and wild when I walked out into the paddock to catch her. I had to spend considerable moments talking gently with her while this ancient horse-girl fear crept over me, then softly slid away. She settled, I climbed into the saddle, and we rode through the warmth of the most beautiful day. Molly trotted faithfully by her side as an unexpected companion joined us and led the way. A pretty blue butterfly danced knowingly above Jessie's muzzle. I went forward in time in this moment. I saw that my mare and I had healed. I could see into our bodies, into our hearts. This indeed would be another kind of special ride.

His wings came out again and like a graceful swan Blue Jeans leapt into the air. I could hear the harmonies carried behind us from the melodic voices of the Angels and the funny play on *Country Roads Take Me Home*, made me laugh and smile and laugh again, as my hair flew about wildly in an etheric breeze. I was taking in every single moment I had left—of the feelings I had, the images I saw and this magical, transcendental happening that had just taken place.

'I love you Bron. I will never leave you.'

The tears were pouring down my cheeks now like steady rain on a lonely window. I felt so much love and so much pain, all in my heart, all churned up together. I did not want to leave *The Pastures*. I belonged there. I believed that I really belonged there.

Then, I remembered people that I loved, my daughter, my family, my friends, my horse Jess, Auntie Shanti, Molly, Tigger and the easy, natural, rustic feeling of the mountain I lived on. I was overwhelmed with love for them all. I did not see them as I had before. Now everyone and everything appeared to be so much more. They were spirits. We were all spirits. We were all from The Light. How long had I been gone?

I had an impression that words were being spoken to me, but they would somehow come up later in my memory. Last words, important things, he was filling my spirit with something and he knew that as we left *The Pastures* I would struggle. I clung so desperately to his neck like a forsaken child. His child.

I heard strong hooves slide confidently into the ground before my tired old body that was still lying unaware and undisturbed in the grass. I was not dead; I knew that instantly. I had collapsed from physical exhaustion—the days and nights of battling Covid. I had fallen into a deep sick-girl sleep.

I could sense that I was indeed very ill, like so many had been, but I had not succumbed to this thing. I had been fighting it. I wanted my body back, but I knew that it came at an immeasurable cost. Claiming my body meant that I would leave the beautiful reality I was now in. I really did not want this dream to end. I did not want to let go of it. I began to protest, but it was futile.

I stood with him for a while, looking at my physical self and then looking back at him, into his soft liquid eyes, into his soul. I took a precious photograph from my heart. Elijah Blue Jeans will forever be with me. He nodded slowly one more time, then disappeared as if he had never ever arrived.

There was dirt in my mouth and my body felt twisted and sore. I lay on the ground for a while, feeling its heaviness and its incredible living beauty all in one. How fortunate was I to be alive, to have a pulse, a heartbeat, a breath? I gently pushed myself up to a sitting position, my mind still very light, with every bone echoing the taxing effects of recent chills and fever. I knew I would not forget one detail of where I had just been and there was something else, I understood in this moment, so clearly and so deeply.

I had no idea how I would start, but I wanted to turn my farm into a physical replica of the beautiful Pastures I had just seen. I wanted to reach from my heart to horses I did not know, horses that needed immediate help and care. I wanted to walk amongst them, listen and learn and heal. I knew this now and finally, completely and unexpectedly, from my unchecked memory of this peculiar afternoon collapse, I understood the *why* in the story of Blue Jeans.

Chapter 15
The Caretaker

I left her there in that special place, a structure I will hold dear in my heavenly heart for all eternity. The dried out, splintered railings, the posts that were loose and bent in the wake of summer itch and the circle the yard formed that symbolized the return for all things. She had not expected me. I see this time and time again. She still does not know that I was with her for three short months, planted lovingly inside her little black colt. They never fully recognize Me and the stories we will share and live, they can only know at the time to be in them, wholly, when love calls.

If a Keeper opens their heart and mind to everything, then everything, even the things that seem impossible, may race towards them in those times when they cry out for answers. My Bron had her answer because she was ready to receive it—she just kept asking *why*. She was ready to step inside the bigger picture ... My dream.

There is a most astounding community project taking place within Creation. We are all a part of it. You, Me, the horses, the humans, the dogs, cats, mountains and oceans, the planets, the stars, the sun and the last blush of moonlight before dawn. We have our missions, our most important stories to live and to share. Each spirit serves the other, we serve each other. This is how I planned it. This is how I made it. For my girl from a mountain farm, I thought of the most glorious horse-loving story and I pulled out all the stops to make it happen. It had good parts and it had amazing parts—it also had some extremely hard parts. It was real, it was alive, it is alive still.

I am always travelling. I love to meet your family, your friends, visit your cozy homes, your city apartments, your mountain fields and your desert plains. But mostly, I just love to encounter hearts, new and old. I like to check in on their durability, their diameters. I collect them, preen them, and protect them like the fine feathers of my mysterious wings.

It is your heart that calls to Me and to your dreaming, blooming, joyful, breaking and suffering heart, I will respond. Without fail, I will turn up. You may never realize who I am, you may just see that you lived a sad story, or a gathered a sweet memory, tripped over an odd clunk on the path of time. But dear reader, let me tell you, when you do see Me, when you know down to the deepest, darkest corners of your life-walking shoes, that I was with you, you will never ever be quite the same.

With love great things can happen. With lots of the same kind of formula, truly miraculous things can happen, for My love is supernatural. Every tear you may have cried precedes a new pool of hope and purpose. All the ideas you have once held, unexpectedly add up to something. They claim a perfect landing place in your life, one you may have peeped at, but not yet inhabited. Challenges that once shook you up, gradually begin to make sense to you. They bear the tools you will need to flourish. The riddle of life and death can no longer hinder the weary when every minute of your day begins to count.

Give to others so generously as you go about life, remember grace. Try and look for ways through things, forgive. Love each other ever so deeply.

For, the song that I sing to you *My beloved* is very simple.

It goes like this …

The contents of your heart are needed somewhere.

Chapter 16
The Fifth Miracle

I believed that this was where I would end the story of my beautiful colt but there was more to share. The experience of life with Blue Jeans was not over. I cannot publish this book without relaying all events and so what I communicate with you now is not so easy to write as it really cannot be fully explained. It is, however, absolute truth and an important part of the story, occurring three days after I had taken that special first ride back on my mare, Jessie.

It was around three a.m. and deep into my sleep, I felt the bedroom shaking as if an earthquake was occurring somewhere and I was experiencing some distant effect. I was sleeping in my daughter's room because I had just begun painting my own room in a different wall color. I wanted a pink room and had found a paint called dusty rose, that suited the feelings I had both creatively and emotionally.

This shaking sensation carried over to my daughter's bed and I began to feel panic inside and opened my eyes. Hovering two feet above me, I glimpsed a gigantic mass of dense white energy. It was vibrating, pulsing and it caused the iron bed ends to clatter. I thought that I might have been about to experience a psychic attack, something I was well used to encountering now and then throughout my years and I began the prayers that I knew would protect me and move an unwanted entity on. But I did not feel fear for long.

As I looked up at this heavy mass above me, a tiny head poked its way through the side to look back at me. It was the head of a foal and then the cloud tore open. The foal fell heavily onto the end of the bed. I must have stepped out of my body at this point. I reached over to touch the foal and it was Blue Jeans. He was tiny, maybe a day old, the way I remembered him from that time. His coat was a deep sorrel colour and I checked the smudged four-leaf clover star on his forehead. I could smell him and I could feel the warmth of his blood beneath his skin. He was alive and his beautiful, unaffected, long colt legs were stretched out across the startled ruffles of an old home-made quilt. It took my breath away. I stroked his little baby face, kissed his eyelids and told him so clearly how much I missed him. He curled the crest of his neck under my chin and the warm breath from his muzzle registered in my heart. I was aware that something extraordinary was happening, but I was also aware that it would only last a few minutes. We had some time. Some special, special time.

There was no mistaking this horse. He had come back to me again and this time, it felt more real than I can truly begin to explain. I have never had a horse sit on my bed, let alone a horse that I had been grieving and crying for, for so long. I did not feel sad for one minute. I felt this immense joy inside me. Whichever way he came into the room, appeared to be some grand Heavenly secret to me. But something, somebody did allow this. Something far greater than I could comprehend.

I was not dreaming. I was fully alert and awake. I was experiencing a vision or a happening that had made its way to the house that I live in, on a quiet little mountain that had not been smiling for some time. Now there was music and wonder filtering through every crack in our picture. A miracle was taking place. Blue Jeans was warm, alive, loving and so happy to have made this journey back. For that brief unexpected moment, he was my baby colt again. But not the same baby I pulled from my mare. This little fella had a story inside him, almost identical to the one that I carried in the ruptured crevice of my heart. He knew. Blue Jeans knew that we had walked through the fire together. The indent his heavy horse body made on the covers; his beautiful, soft eyes; the heartbeat of him that resounded in his juvenile chest and the smell of his baby horse coat, confirmed his realness to me. I could even touch his whiskers.

What was authentic about him never left me. I never left him. The love between us had been shown to exist in both worlds no matter where the story was up to. I was aware in this moment that Blue Jeans had wanted this time with me. He had been part of making it happen.

When he left the room with the mass of white, I felt complete. I was so happy and so grateful that life brought him back to me in this way. It kept me on high for several weeks later and there is not one aspect of that unpredicted moment with him I can ever forget. I wanted to tell everyone I knew, and I did tell a few. But no matter how I tried, I could not communicate in spoken words, the full detail of the experience. It was as if Heaven has this filter. We can sound like fools on Earth, but we are not. We are all just listeners and learners. There is no way I could ever believe this did not happen and I want the world to know about it. God reaches out to us. He really does ... and He has this truly mind-blowing bag of tricks up His sleeve.

Life is both cruel and merciful. Blue Jeans has been missing from our mountain but not from our dreams, our visions, or our hearts—not even from the end of the bed. I was given more time. As I reflected on every challenge we faced together, it seemed that time was the very thing that continued to extend. Time after a traumatic birth; time after two fractured bones; time after a gruesome hole in the back; time after deathly colic and now, time after physical death. Each extension of time presented to me as a succession of miracles.

A miracle is defined as an event that cannot be explained by natural or scientific laws and is attributed to some higher supernatural cause or intervention. I fought so hard inside my heart not to sink into oblivion when everything looked so hopeless. This was because of him. He was a baby horse and I was responsible for his welfare.

Perhaps the miracle is already living within us, planted there, just in case. Yes, faith certainly helps and prayers never go astray, but what is it that holds us together when the very worst is unfolding before our lives and we cannot stop it.

We become the miracle, I think, because we turn up and we try to find a way, even though we may lose all hope and we may suffer. He was the dream and the wish for the story of my heart. One thing became exceedingly clear to me as I thought lovingly back on the days spent with my beautiful black colt with the unmissable white wings. There had been this lost piece to the puzzle. Something quite striking about this little fella that I just could not figure until it was staring me blatantly and extremely patiently in the face. He was Blue Jeans, yes, but he was much more than that.

He was God in action, God amongst us, God planted firmly in my heart, and when I saw that and I grasped that, I did not have to lose Him ever again.

Chapter 17
The Unforeseen

There were so many times when I felt his presence around our farm. Blue Jeans turned up in two more photos that were taken during times when I was really missing him. In the collection of feathers, I placed in a pink teacup, a striking blue feather came through on film with an image of his face contrasted on a small grey feather alongside it. How could this be happening? His face and beautiful eyes were unmistakable.

Then on Mother's Day, I came home and found a faint white wing painted on the screen of my bedroom window. I do not know how it got there but I thought of him immediately and decided to take a photo. In this unexpected snap, set just under the wing, is the image of my colt superimposed onto the trunk of a tree that stands dutifully outside the window. He was there. His spirit was there in the moment I reached for my phone to capture something that had suddenly turned my heart— an unexplainable brush of white paint in the shape of a wing.

I cannot prove or rationalize any of these things, only to state unequivocally that they really happened.

They were very real occurrences. But something else that surprised me amongst it all, was that my grief continued to pour out of my soul like some haphazard spew of sustained sadness. There seemed to be no reprieve from it at times. I was overjoyed with his spiritual presence in my life, I had uncovered the truth of Him, but still suffering from the horrible loss. Surely, I should be happy and healed by now. I just wasn't.

One night I went out with my mother to watch my brother play his music at a local venue. I was having a great time sitting and listening to songs that urged your body to go and tear up a floor but discovered I could not dance. No amount of coaxing from the inside or the outside, was going to get me into something I usually love to do. My mother stated rather resolutely that it was because my legs were tied to his. I could not use my legs for fun while I was still suffering the breakdown of the colt's legs. On some very hidden and practical level it made sense. I could not pick up my guitar and sing either.

Grief and mourning take time. My legs felt paralyzed that night I was with my family. A good friend of mine reminded me, that feeling stuck in such a way, means you are not meant to move just yet. Trust that.

I just missed him so much. My mind flicks from his birth, his face, the stables, the round yard, the needle, the grave, the photos, the special ride into Heavenly pastures, the visit at the end of the bed. That is a flaming big story! Each segment is embedded tightly within me like a cherished diamond. He is my soul. He is my heart and soul. What is missing in me? Innocence, beauty, trust? I just do not know where to go with it at times. How do I process it all? Am I supposed to let go? I do not want to.

At the time of this ongoing grieving, Blue Jeans would have been just over seven months old, weaned from his dam and ready for more *one on one* time in training. How much closer would we have grown on Earth as horse and human? I still have this unshakeable feeling that he will appear. That his physical presence will be returned to me, not only the spiritual make-up of him. Seeing him after death has been amazing, yet it can also make no sense at all, to a girl who longs for her horse. Thoughts of Horse Heaven remain overwhelmingly clear, beautiful, mystical, surreal but then the paddock at home looks empty each day.

Sometimes I find myself questioning life in a new and interesting way. Has this odd thing ever happened on Earth? I wonder? Does God throw humans a super wild card every now and then? Does He decide that the death was not the best outcome, even though it never truly is the end? Does He make blunders and then corrects them? Can the Heavens give a baby back, give a foal back to its Keeper because their heart just does not operate the same without them?

Is this the *unforeseen* calling to all my tormented sensitivities? Am I clutching at straws? I do not feel full closure yet. Is my imagination taking me way beyond a safe little boundary of beliefs? Maybe it is just a matter of time. I feel guilty for wanting more when I have been given so much.

He turned up in yet another photo. The golden light of Heaven made its way to the far corner of a tiny paddock I had built around his grave. It never occurred to me that he would be there, but he was. When I zoom in on the light, there is his beautiful face looking back at me.

Amazing. Just amazing. He wants to be seen. He whispers to me on the inside. He encourages me to take a closer look. I feel humbled by these moments and when I find him in the background, my spirit soaks itself in happiness.

I have a lot of stories in my past that have been wonderful and hard and beautiful and testing, but nothing has affected me in such a way as this experience with Blue Jeans ... of going from *Birth to Death* in three months, then *Death to Life After Death*, for the next four.

I have buried many adored pets on the mountain and lost friends and family to death. I am not unfamiliar with a grieving process, but I have never felt a loss so caught in confusion and desperation as the one I am feeling right now. Like the silent flickering of an old black and white film my heart is running pictures, constantly telling his story.

I miss him so much. I miss him so much.

Perhaps I am being very selfish. Maybe my little colt is far happier in Heaven. He could even have other people here on Earth that he is meant to find. It is not my call at all where he should be, and I must keep setting something free. I would give anything to have him in my life in the physical sense, but I do have him somewhere.

There were more tears to cry and then one evening a visit in my prayers from my savior. Lord Jesus was smiling at me and telling me that all was exactly as it was meant to be. He was holding something with such tenderness as he looked softly into my eyes with His trademark brand of Divine love.

'I have your foal, Bron.'

The little black colt was carefully cradled in His arms. Happy, content, loved. It brought me so much peace to see him there, held, hugged, safe—I guess as safe as he will ever be. Then quite unexpectedly, The Lord handed Blue Jeans to me, as one would pass a baby. He smiled into my nature and with the greatest warmth and affection He said,

'I am giving him back.'

I wondered if I had imagined this part. Was I just wishful thinking here in amongst prayer and meditation? Then I figured two things.

One was that well, let's face it, if I imagined this conversation, I imagined a foal falling onto my bed, a trip to Heaven from a round yard and gasp, two perfect white wings discovered on the back of a baby horse on a sweet country night. I imagined a traumatic birth, two fractured bones, a hole in the back, a deathly colic and a sinister syringe. Nope, I did not imagine any of those things.

Then two, well, if The Lord is giving him back, maybe Blue Jeans has been really naughty in the Heavenly Realms. Maybe he bit somebody.

I called this chapter *The Unforeseen* because I just cannot see what is coming, yet beyond any doubts or confusion, I can feel that there is something more. It is rarely what we may think or hope for, the details we might imagine for our lives often pale in comparison when it comes to His ideas and plans for us. I want to know, but I cannot. I need patience and faith. I want to sit down with the General Manager in His office, sip a hot, brewed chai and say, 'Nice to see you, thank you for absolutely everything, what is on the agenda?'

I am sure that my ongoing questioning had already really worn the patience of something somewhere. If you feel there is more, then clearly, that is because there is. A very well prepared, twinkling *something* is standing back quite selflessly in the pleats of time, just waiting to bump into you.

I would not describe myself as a religious person, even though I have the greatest respect for all religions and beliefs that come from love and that reach to love. The story of my spiritual life has led me to spend time in different faiths for a period, to learn loving principles, to find God again and to appreciate the common ground.

The relationship I have with The Caretaker is personal and very simple. I feel closest to Him when I am in nature. I feel close when I am near a horse.

I wondered why Blues Jeans was called Elijah. His Heavenly name was still a mystery to me, yet I knew there was the Good Book of research available, so I opened it.

Elijah was a prophet who stayed faithful to God. He was a messenger of God and performed eight miracles during his time on Earth, including bringing a woman's son back to life. He did not physically die at the end of his time; he was taken straight to Heaven in a chariot of fire. There is much more to his story than this, but these are the parts that really stood out for me.

When I heard the words *'Are you ready?'* in *The Pastures*, I was confused. Ready for what? Only time has shown me that God was saying so much more to me from every other direction. When I paid attention to my life, I could see and hear His constant communications.

I believe Elijah Blue Jeans had a clear idea of the message he was delivering to our farm. He was meek, he never complained about the pain he was in and such a strong example of Heavenly love in this world. The Caretaker must have really thought this story through. How could He teach me lessons in a way where I would keep on reaching for more? I believe that from the birth to the death of a beautiful black colt, He chose a language and a prophet that would most certainly wake me up.

Chapter 18
Treasure

Time went for a long stroll around the gardens. Roses turned to wood yet still managed to bloom, lavender wafted selflessly through the bedroom windows and lantana dominated every single natural space it could possibly claim. Without any warning, I experienced the guilty threads of the truly unthinkable. I went for a whole week where my attention suddenly lifted from a little colt's grave and all the sadness of the past, to focus on something else.

I came across an exotic, handsome and rare face on a dating app. You know, the kind of face that looked and felt like home. Fortunately, this face, had the same feeling towards my face and an instant connection was made by the click of a button and the sweet, celebratory beep of technology. Matchmaking tools had succeeded, finally! I wondered if back at dating app headquarters, people actually broke out the streamers and champagne.

Joaquin was very different to any man I had ever met before through a phone screen. He wanted to know all about Blue Jeans and his legs. With compassion and interest, I felt a friendship building as a new human story unfolded before me. He also wanted to know about me and I had no problem sharing stories with this stranger, trusting that each precious fragment of my life was tumbling into very safe hands.

He was from America doing a three-month locum in Newcastle, a city three hours from where I live. As an orthopedic surgeon, he could explain to me fully, why the little colt's legs broke down in the way that they did. Amongst thoughtful texting, he was fixing, saving, rushing to emergencies of all different kinds of broken bones and body. He was somebody I trusted with my secret voice, yet we had not even met in person. There was this warmth about him—he knew from a very young age that he wanted to save lives.

Why didn't I know something like that when I was young? I was so busy back then daydreaming about Blue Jeans on a tree branch, in my old faded levis and grubby green t-shirt. I felt something from Joaquin, that I had not felt in a long time. A person who genuinely cared about how I was going through my day. These were statements and accounts I often filled in for myself as I lay in bed each night and talked to the walls. I had someone to check in with and as I unexpectedly realized, when the text return was delayed, someone else to miss.

Joaquin was supportive of my plans for horse rescue on the farm. He upheld my dreams as if they were his very own, offering ideas for how to begin. He wanted to open an orthopedic clinic, so I guess we were kindred spirits in some way. I wished he had been in my life when Blue Jeans was born, but he was in my life now. Maybe the Angels had sent me a human that could help with the emotional load and the final processing part. Maybe he will only pass through my life briefly. The questions inside were building rapidly when really, all I needed to do was just *live* and forget about trying to figure everything out.

He was just passing through. How odd? We never met in person, but I was grateful for the small amount of time we had in cyber space connection and communication. He offered a very timely distraction and sent an invaluable message my way. *It was okay to start living and loving again.*

There is an impermanence to life that we can really count on, and I had no desire to let it dampen my path from here. I was changing.

So, I made that choice. I signed up for joy. The celebration of coming back to life, really outdid itself. I bought myself a brand-new car, cut my hair in what can only be described as a *Nikita the Sexy Spy* bob and upgraded my dismal wardrobe. I even invested time creating French manicures in varying degrees of success, on my somewhat chipped and alarmed country nails. I learned how to use a hair straightener and a hair curler! I was a long way from shoveling horse shit and I knew it. I took pleasure in giving attention to myself, while the farm nodded gleefully and rather considerately in approval. Somewhere down deep, I felt that Blue Jeans would be happy about all this. Maybe he was just standing behind me, snorting the air in delight, secretly beaming the sweetness of his soul.

I went out one night to our welcoming country hall to listen to travelling musicians. They were visiting small towns all over Australia, offering their time and acoustic talent as an emotional antidote from droughts, fires, floods and Covid. *The Festival of Small Halls* entertained a group of very cheery and hungry country folk. We had not seen a local concert, let alone each other in such a long time. There was this one song, with the words ... *I'm going to let you love me* ... well, it got me fair in the heartstrings and made some kind of perfect uncommon sense. I knew I had plans to finish this writing, build more paddocks, plant sunflowers for spring in the tiny yard around Blue Jeans' grave. I also knew that there was this new chapter of life, pleading with me to just walk forward.

I sat on my swinging chair that looks straight down the Valley and thought back on the sweetest summer night—all that followed, all that was lost ... and all that returned. I sipped on such a wonderous memory through a most perfectly positioned cup of tea—deliberately blocking out all the hard bits. They were there, but they had somehow become soft and faded. I wanted to remember his tiny black face, all wet and sticky as I tore open the holy sac that brought him to me.

And you know, there are these sensitive folk that are amongst us. Girls and boys that love animals in ways so deep, the atoms of life inside them almost burst in that knowledge. I met a young horse girl recently and she was numb to the core, just like I had been. Saddened and shocked by the departure of her whole heart, her beloved horse. That is what happens you know. A big animal that you have loved and who loves you back, will occupy your soul in ways that cannot be matched by anything—I am very sure that it is the same for any fur family friend.

Horses are not cruel or manipulative. They are patient, honest and present—wild as can be at times, but pure of heart and willing to let us in. We are given privilege and opportunity by this gesture. Can we be relied upon? Can we be trusted to return to a horse exactly what they ask of us? Enduring love, someone they can depend upon. They ask this from their paddocks and they keep on asking, long after they have left us.

In death they leave an almighty gap, an extraction of the heart.

They become *The Keepers* of that treasure and because it lives within, they remember us and do all that they can to find their way back somehow—whatever that means; a dream; a story; a miracle ... *I call my heart back to me.*

They do not want us to suffer for too long. They understand our sadness because they are feeling it too. They hope that we remember them. We hope that they remember us. It is as if a deal has been struck, just like when two horses align themselves at the gate, nipping at each other's manes and shoulders, answering the plea of each other's nagging itch in such perfect unison. We itch and we ache for what has filled us so completely.

If a horse has inhabited our soul, then their image lives within us forever, in those warm, velvety places … never to be disturbed. And just like fine china, they wait patiently upon the little shelves of childhood dreams and the mountains of grown-up sorrow… while the fractured, broken bits are all put back together.

I looked out my bedroom window and Blue Jeans was there, standing strong and proud near my father's rose garden, waiting for me to notice him. His coat was strikingly different this time—a rich, russet red.

THE END